ADVANCE PRAISE

"Pushing boundaries and redefining limits is what I live for, and *Fit for Wealth* embodies that spirit. Chad bridges the gap between health and wealth, showing that excellence in one can elevate the other. This book is a game-changer for those striving for peak performance in every area of life!"

— JAMES LAWRENCE, THE IRON COWBOY, ENDURANCE WORLD RECORD HOLDER

"Health and wealth are part of the same system for successful people. If you don't take care of both of them at the same time, neither will get you very far! Chad's book *Fit for Wealth* is perfectly timed because of recent technology breakthroughs. Put health and wealth together, and you can get a second entrepreneurial lifetime that's 1,000 times bigger than the other one, allowing you to take new risks, set bigger goals, and have more confidence."

— DAN SULLIVAN, CO-FOUNDER OF STRATEGIC COACH, BESTSELLING CO-AUTHOR OF *WHO NOT HOW, THE GAP AND THE GAIN,* & *10X IS EASIER THAN 2X*

"When it comes to the delicate balance of work, life, family, spirit, and wealth, Chad Willardson has the full game 100% decoded. If you are serious about life fitness that goes way beyond just your abs and muscles, this book is for you."

— BEN GREENFIELD, CEO & FOUNDER OF BEN GREENFIELD LIFE, CO-FOUNDER OF KOIN

"Health is wealth. Most people think you have to sacrifice one for the other, but you don't! Chad is the best in the business at teaching how to grow your wealth and improve your health! The guy is living the dream and teaching from real-life experience! This book is a must-read."

— DAVID NURSE, *WSJ* BEST SELLING AUTHOR, TOP 50 WORLDWIDE KEYNOTE SPEAKER, MINDSET & MENTAL SKILLS SPECIALIST

"*Fit for Wealth* is a must-read for anyone looking to surpass previous versions of personal and professional success. Not only does Chad layout the process to accomplish unreasonable health and wealth, but he backs it up with real-life experience. I found his willingness to be vulnerable in sharing his personal experience in his own health journey inspiring."

— REGAN ARCHIBALD, FMP, LAC, LONGEVITY EXPERT

FIT FOR WEALTH

FIT
FOR
WEALTH

7 Breakthrough Strategies for
Elite Health and Abundant Wealth

CHAD WILLARDSON, CRPC®, AWMA®

ISBN
979-8-89165-043-5 *Paperback*
979-8-89165-044-2 *Hardback*
979-8-89165-045-9 *Ebook*

www.strategiccoach.com

To my wife Amber, whose personal dedication to her fitness and health has never wavered (when we first met, she was working out intensely twice each day, and I remember being so impressed and inspired).

To my five children—McKinley, Pierce, Sterling, Bentley and Beckham—who are the constant source of my inspiration and motivation to be my best, and whom I hope to inspire to always live a life of making great choices.

To my personal trainer Ryan Stevens and John Madsen and his company Supra Human, for pushing me to reach my ambitious health goals and stay consistent.

To my friends and peers, whose own big goals and dreams have really enriched each page of this journey. This book is a testament to all of you—my tribe. Here's to our shared pursuit of fitness, in body and wealth.

Cheers to every challenge we've faced and every triumph we've celebrated together on the journey to living an elite lifestyle that only comes through hard work and extreme discipline. 'Fit for Wealth' is as much yours as it is mine.

CONTENTS

FOREWORD
IN CONVERSATION WITH DAN SULLIVAN

I was fortunate enough to get an interview with friend and mentor, Dan Sullivan—co-founder and president of Strategic Coach, author of forty-six books, and widely considered the top entrepreneur coach in the world—to gather his wisdom on the correlation between creating elite health and abundant wealth. Not surprisingly, he had a lot to share.

Chad: *Let's start with the big picture: connecting health and wealth.*

Dan: *For me, it starts with thinking about what is the 'what' of life and what is the 'why' of life. You can't answer one without the other because health and wealth are actually part of the same system for people who are successful. It doesn't matter how much money you have or where you are, but if you don't take* care of both of them at the same time, neither will get you very far. I've seen a lot of people who have gotten very wealthy, but at the sacrifice of their health, right? So they end up with a lot of money at a certain point, but then all their money goes to repair the damage they did along the way. And that's not very satisfying.

Chad: *That's so true.*

Dan: *Yeah, and part of the reason is that your physical health and energy level is really the source of what you find enjoyable in life. And this is a good book for right now because there have been breakthroughs in both health and wealth because of the digital economy.*

Chad: *I agree. So much of wealth now is being generated in ideas. One of the main areas where the internet has produced extraordinary results is AI.*

Dan: *Yes. One application of AI is regenerative medicine that can now go down to the cellular level and repair damage. You can essentially grow new supports for your existing organs. We're on the path now where you can basically take yourself backwards. For example, I'll be seventy-nine in four months. Babs and I (who is my wife, my partner in life and business) have invested about $3 million since 1985 just looking at different testing opportunities and therapies and procedures. Some of 'em worked, and some of 'em didn't work. But you've got to try, right? And we were only able to invest that in our health because we had that $3 million. That's where the wealth part comes in. There are amazing opportunities to use both great health and wealth to extend your life and* *your time in the entrepreneurial world, which is the only world I live in, right?*

Chad: *Makes sense.*

Dan: *Say you're sixty right now and not healthy. Then, you have one goal in life: to hold on for as long as possible. But say you're sixty and really healthy, and you're at the top of your wealth creation right now. What would it mean if you had another thirty years at the top of your game? Put health and wealth together, and all of the sudden, you're getting a second entrepreneurial lifetime that's 1,000 times bigger than the other one. And you're enjoying it then, too. Your body agrees that you should go and take new risks, set bigger goals, and have more confidence. I don't think you have intellectual, psychological, and emotional confidence unless you have physical energy.*

Chad: *That's interesting. Talk more about that.*

Dan: *Yeah. Basically, I believe your body won't let you risk your past if your past is the only thing you have. For example, I have a family member who is in a particular field of engineering and technology. He is really, really well known across the world. We were at a family gathering and went out for drinks afterwards, and we started to talk a bit. I'm used to dealing with entrepreneurs, so I can usually pull out what an entrepreneur is doing uniquely. And I could see he had some really unique ideas. I told him he should push for growth, and he said he just didn't have the fire in the belly anymore for that. He said, 'I can't do that now; it's a young man's game.' He's seven or eight years older than me now, but he had pioneering work that he could've started on twenty* *years ago that he just didn't because he didn't have the physical energy.*

Chad: *That's a great example. So what mindsets help you create significant wealth and optimal health? What are those common mindsets?*

Dan: *Three things: growth, growth, and growth (laughs). That game you just won or the deal you just made might be the biggest so far, but it's also just a starting point for the next stage of growth. I'm more ambitious at almost seventy-nine than I was thirty years ago. But I'm also in better physical health now than I was then. It's incredible. The tests prove it... If I had this testing in 1980, I'd be even wealthier (laughs). But I have a lot of energy. We're up 260 times bigger than we were our first year, and we continue to make significant jumps. I've taken one whole area of coaching that I've done for ten years, a really big money-maker and everything, and said 'it's time for other people to take over because I'm ready for something new.'*

Chad: *How do you build that courage to keep growing and challenging yourself? What about that person who is sixty-five, has a lot of money, is kind of healthy and feels like they're winding down, whereas you're almost seventy-nine and setting bigger goals than you ever have before. Where does that come from?*

Dan: *Well, part of it is factory equipment. I do think ambition is a capability that you can develop very simply: you just keep setting goals that scare you, right? And they're not foolish goals. They're achievable within a time period... I usually use two to three years as the time period, but you can make your own. That means chal-*

lenging yourself, leaving some things behind—same for the health and wealth side. You have to be willing to make yourself coachable from people who are really doing breakthrough work. Whatever they tell you, you have to do it if you want change.

Chad: *What are some breakthroughs you've had?*

Dan: *The biggest one for me is resistance training because both your mental and physical health really depend on muscle, so you have to keep that ratio up in your body. I'm not in the top one percent of physical health for all men, but I'd be in the top one percent for seventy-eight-year-olds. Same for wealth: I'm in the top one percent. I've always seen the two as going together from the very beginning. And I have to give a lot of credit to Babs, because I was on a downward path when I met her in the eighties. I was drinking too much and just eating inappropriately. Going through the motions of exercise without it really sticking. And she pointed out that you have to keep your brain in great shape, because if that's not happening, it's going to show up as some deficiency.*

Chad: *What are some things you do to keep your brain in shape?*

Dan: *Well, entrepreneurship puts you in a good space. If you've created your own company, that company is a great protector of your health for many reasons. You have obligations to people beyond yourself. To your team, customers, people who work for you. That means you're someone who likes to take on responsibility. And also, you know when to rest. Babs and I take the equivalent of around twenty weeks a year of free time, mostly a couple weeks at a time. Resting is so important—and so is sleep.*

Chad: *Speaking of the value of rest, let's look at what feels like the opposite of that. What is your approach to stress?*

Dan: *Well, there's good stress and bad stress. I mean, your body needs stress because it provides resistance. And your muscles can only grow if you give 'em resistance. Your brain is the same. You need a certain amount of psychological and emotional stress because it forces your attention and helps you sort out what's important. But you can't over stress.*

Chad: *What helps with that?*

Dan: *Most entrepreneurs in the program are somewhere between forty and sixty. If they're forty, they're not as strong as they were at thirty, right? They have less muscle. They're probably not sleeping well. And that's the biggest thing, especially with this group: they don't sleep well. Sleep has a universal impact on your health. Every part of you depends on the quality of it, too. There's REM, deep... all of that restorative sleep... that you can't get in just six hours a night. I can tell you that. It's universally understood that you need at least eight hours of sleep. People may say, 'well, I've trained myself to get by on five.' And I say, 'you aren't fooling anyone but yourself.' (laughs)*

Chad: *Yeah, that's counterintuitive because some hustle culture says you've got to be out there at all hours working on your business.*

Dan: *You're right. But that's not true. I mean, you can do that, but then you're going to burn out and die. And look, there is idiosyncrasy, sure. Everybody is put together differently. Our nervous systems are put together differently. That's why I do testing. We* have the general information, but the testing and technology helps us move the needle. It's like... how long could your body really last if you took care of it?'

Chad: *It's the same with money.*

Dan: *Exactly. Money is a really interesting thing. You've got to have real meaning for your money. I've seen a lot of wealthy people who have way, way more money than they have meaning.*

Chad: *Can you explain what you mean by that?*

Dan: *You need to have a goal for your money. For example, Babs and I have enough money that if the company made no income for an entire year, we could cover it. Nobody would have to be fired or anything. And that became really important during COVID because, first, our entire income stream was taken away because we do live workshops. So our future income stream was gone, almost instantly. The company takes $20 million to $28 million or something. And we're at about forty. And we didn't beat an eyelash when this happened. We wanted our team to know they would be taken care of.*

Chad: *But you didn't give up.*

Dan: *Not at all. We said, 'I guess we're going to have to experiment with Zoom.' In two or three months, we completely reconfigured the company and went entirely to Zoom. And now, two years later, we're right back to where we were before but our profits are better. The basic idea here is that you can't create the wealth you want without a number, and you can't create the health you want without the numbers. And those numbers can be negotiable, but* they need to be there. When we first started, we were in the hundreds of thousands of dollars for year one. And now, our goal for the next three years is $75 million.

Chad: *So, that's the number. Wow.*

Dan: *Yeah. And I know we've got entrepreneurs who are way smaller or way bigger than us, so they're going to have a different number. There's no self-comparison here. I've got people who are fifty years younger than me in the program, and they're making moves. It's a pleasure for me to download all my years of experiences and lessons and say, 'I have to tell you... don't give death or the tax department any assistance.'*

Chad: *I love that. Because that's exactly what this book is for, too.*

INTRODUCTION

On November 2, 2022, around 11:30 p.m., on the twenty-seventh floor of the Hyatt Hotel in Denver, Colorado, I came to a very discouraging realization: my personal health was a mess. The exact moment it hit me was a total wake-up call that's etched into my memories. Four members of my Pacific Capital team and I were in the Peaks Lounge on the top floor of a high-rise—all windows, an incredible view of the city lights. There was a live band playing for the first night of the annual industry conference hosted by Charles Schwab, the largest such event for wealth managers. My team and I were there at the conference with a crowd of more than five thousand people from all over the country. After a packed schedule of meetings, mingling, and attending the conference kickoff sessions, I felt fortunate to attend this premier private party overlooking Denver at night.

That day, there'd been a tremendous amount of energy on the

floor, as people circulated among the investment booths. The world was just reopening after COVID-19—the conference had been canceled three years in a row—and this was the first major event most of us had attended. There was also non-stop access to incredible food; everywhere you looked, the conference showcased different top-notch local restaurants, and I'd been eating straight through... enjoying all the goodness. I'd been traveling a lot recently and hadn't kept my appetite under control, and tonight would be the night it would all stop for me.

Though I was already stuffed from a delicious dinner at Fleming's Steakhouse, this afterparty gave me a second wind. I saw the chefs preparing great food, including some juicy barbecue bacon cheeseburger sliders. Yes, cheeseburgers, but they were special—from a well-known Denver barbecue restaurant. When in Denver, of course I had to try this gourmet comfort food. I went over and grabbed one or three.

I returned to our round table, where I was sitting with the team from Pacific Capital and four other people we were mingling with. Some of the guys from my team said, "Man, you're going all out. How are you still hungry?"

I had a moment of realizing I probably was not very hungry, and I questioned myself. *What was I doing?* However, I was at a special event, and felt like treating myself... and I wanted to enjoy the work of these famous local chefs. As I took another bite, the slider dripped the delicious sauce and bacon grease onto my shirt. I quickly wiped it off before the guys saw it, but something didn't feel right to me and I knew it.

In that moment, I saw that I'd completely lost self-control of my health habits. I used to be an accomplished athlete, and love the beach, so there's some vanity about looking good in a swimsuit. What had happened to me? How'd I let myself go like this? I didn't even recognize myself.

One of the people at our table recognized me from LinkedIn, knew I'd written books before, and asked me a question that helped put in motion why you're reading this exact book today:

"Hey Chad, are you planning on writing any more books or are you done at three?"

"Yes, actually, my goal is to write ten books in ten years."

"Nice. What's the next one going to be about?"

"I'm not sure, but I've been really thinking about the correlation and alignment between building wealth and creating incredible health."

My friends gave me a look, and even some laughs and some teasing, as I scarfed another bite of my bacon cheeseburger. "Yeah," they said, "the guy who's sitting here wolfing down bacon cheeseburger sliders at midnight is going to write the book on creating optimal physical health."

None of that teasing was given with malintent. They work for me and they're also personal friends of mine, so we joke around a lot together. But this time it stung a bit. Because it was true. And it's exactly the stinging I needed to decide to make a drastic change.

I set my cheeseburger down and said, "Yes, I am going to write that book. I'll show you. First I'm going to finish this juicy burger, and then I'll transform my fitness and get myself in incredible shape. And I'm going to write about this exact moment in the introduction of the book about my fitness journey."

The teasing didn't feel great, but it also got me fired up. I realized they might think I couldn't do it, and it was just me talking big. The principles of discipline and habits that create abundant wealth and business success are the same for personal health and fitness. They've seen the one side from me, but never the extreme discipline for fitness. So I decided to show them—and myself.

"Just wait until my birthday [January 31]," I said. "You'll see a different me."

They smiled and the laughter died down, and we moved on to other topics.

But I was serious. They didn't believe I'd follow through, but inside, I was already fully committed. That night, I took a picture of myself in the hotel room with my shirt off to document my starting point. I weighed myself on the hotel scale: 255 pounds, the most I'd ever weighed in my life. I wrote in my journal, "My knees have been sore, I'm embarrassed with my shirt off, and I'm deciding to become the example that I'm going to write about in this next book."

The next day in the conference hall, I was again surrounded by unlimited offerings of delicious pastries and treats. But for the first time in a long time, I refused to indulge.

It was Day One of my journey.

HEALTH TRANSFORMS MORE THAN YOUR BODY

According to an article in *Forbes*, health and wealth are directly correlated.[1] The richest people have fewer health conditions than the upper middle class, who have fewer issues than the lower middle class, and so on. There are foundational principles for good health, including limiting sugar, exercising regularly, and not smoking. Good habits for wealth building include consistently saving and investing, creating passive income, and keeping your spending in check. You're probably familiar with these concepts; what you may not have considered is the extent to which health care and wealth care go hand in hand.

Health and wealth are correlated in a number of ways and share similar principles for growth and maintenance. For instance, they both require you to take consistent action without potentially seeing results for a very long time. They're also both subject to the compounding effect of small, consistent habits. You can't expect to build legacy wealth if you're only careful with your money two weeks out of the month and then blowing the budget the other two weeks. That approach won't work for your health, either. If you eat in moderation and exercise all week but spend the weekend binge eating and chilling on the couch, you'll never reach your peak level of fitness. If you skip exercise or rationalize your "cheat days," you're just making it harder on yourself to become the person you're capable of becoming.

Both health and wealth require consistency, discipline, and follow-through over the long term, without being able to see results right away.

If you can only transform one area of your life, focus on optimizing your personal health—it will, in turn, transform all the other areas of your life for the better. There

are strong correlations among discipline and success, and that discipline expands into every area you can think of.

One thing I've always found fascinating about restaurants or stores is that the customers of those places seem to be very similar to one another. Have you ever noticed that? If you're a greasy barbecue joint, chances are, the customers are totally okay with hammering a 3,000-calorie lunch of barbecue slop sandwiches and french fries and that's their thing. By contrast, people walking into a raw vegan restaurant will find a very different customer base. I'm not saying either one of those is right or wrong, in fact, I'd typically prefer the barbecue sandwich in that case. My point is this: different environments attract different people who share similar mindsets and habits with one another. We make little choices like this every day—and those little choices add up.

Most people in America are not in great financial shape, and they're not in good health shape either. Sixty-one percent of Americans live paycheck-to-paycheck and cannot cover an unexpected emergency expense of $1,000.[2] And maybe even more shocking, two in three Americans are considered over-weight or obese and only one in three adults get the recommended amount of physical activity per week.[3] Sadly, most people don't seem to have support to help break out of the norms that have become so acceptable. It's a lot like the old "crab in the bucket" analogy: crab mentality is a mindset that believes, "if I can't have it, neither can you." The metaphor is derived from the behavior of crabs when they are trapped in a bucket: while any one crab can easily start to climb out, it will usually be pulled back in by the others, ensuring the group's collective demise.

The comparable theory in human behavior says that members of a group will attempt to reduce the self-confidence of any member who achieves success beyond the others, out of envy, jealousy, resentment, spite, conspiracy, or competitive feelings, to halt their progress. In other words, the average person would rather you eat that second (or third) dessert or make that big impulse purchase on the credit card, because it makes them feel better about *their own* lack of discipline. Maybe you've experienced or seen that in your personal life. Once you see it, you can't unsee it. But you've got to see it first before you can transform your life. You need to tap into a mindset of not letting other people set limitations on you or hold you back just because your success makes them uncomfortable.

Wealth = Freedom + Money + Time

The media doesn't help; everything on TV commercials seems perfectly designed to get you to make poorer health decisions and poorer wealth decisions. There are all kinds of offers to buy now and pay later in monthly installments, complete with ridiculously high interest rates. We're bombarded by ads featuring the latest sizzling, greasy fast food and desserts to be delivered right to your doorstep, with pills and medications that will treat whatever consequences come your way.

Society eats so much junk food that eating real food is considered dieting.

There's very little discussion of the "boring" and tough discipline it takes to make you healthy and wealthy. You won't find that advice in all the pop-up ads or videos you scroll through on social media.

But you'll find plenty of it in this book.

YOU'RE DIFFERENT

If you're reading this book, you're unique. You don't just pick up a book about elite health and abundant wealth if you're content to live a mediocre life just going through the motions. Most of my readers and connections are successful entrepreneurs. And if that's you, you've already bucked the system. You're already not normal, not a follower of group think, nor a subscriber of the status quo. As my friend Gino Wickman says, "An entrepreneur is someone who jumps off of a cliff and assembles an airplane on the way down."

If this is you, congratulations on choosing a life of trailblazing your own path, taking big chances and being willing to make adjustments on the fly. What else are you going to do with it?

You've likely reached a level of success where you aren't just working for money, but your money is actually working for you. Your resources and success give you access to cutting-edge approaches and connections to increase both your fitness and your net worth.

You're not the kind of person who blindly follows the crowd, but there's temptation all around us. You might get caught up being a social eater, a social drinker, or even a social spender. In those cases, you justify compromising your long-term goals because you're around others who don't share your standards.

All those exceptions to your rules add up, though. Instead of having endless cheat days, surround yourself with people who share your disciplined mindset. Otherwise, you'll have an ongoing internal struggle and lack of self-confidence. Consider this: five out of seven is seventy-one percent. That's a "C-" grade. If you go off the rails every weekend eating like crap, don't expect to get "A" results. Choosing the easy route instead of what the top 1 percent do, you won't get the results you want and deserve.

Be bold, and don't worry about the judgment or criticism of people who aren't aiming for big goals. You've got a big and exciting future ahead of yourself, one that includes using your success and abundance to live a life of purpose, legacy, and impact. All that's possible when you maximize your healthspan and your financial resources to not only create an incredible lifestyle, but to inspire and uplift others.

REAL CHANGE

Eating that middle-of-the-night bacon cheeseburger with the laughter of some of my friends above the Denver skyline changed my life. It made me really reflect internally about how closely health and wealth are connected. I now believe the focus should be on healthspan, not lifespan. There's so much focus on people's age and how people are living longer. But to me, it's not just about living longer, but living *healthier for longer*. I want to live to be 120 years old, but that's only because I want to still be healthy when I'm 119. I have no desire to be just hanging around, bedridden and hooked up to IVs consumed with doctor's appointments every day, all day.

I told my friends I'd be transformed by my birthday, January 31. Ironically, that's the date by which most people abandon their New Year's resolutions to get fit and healthy every year. By that date, I'd lost forty pounds and looked like a different person. People who hadn't seen me in a few weeks asked, "What the heck are you doing, man?" They told me I looked way younger.

As I write this, I'm down fifty pounds, and am actually stronger and lifting heavier weights than when I weighed more.

How? I went ALL IN. When I look at pictures and videos from last year, I see the extent to which I'd lost control. I don't recognize myself. I'm actually kind of bummed that nobody said anything to me as I got further out of shape than ever before. Like someone spotting food in my teeth, I would've appreciated the blunt observation from a caring friend!

When I had the idea for this book, I knew I couldn't write it unless I first *became* it. My good friend, Dr. Benjamin Hardy, always tells me you have to become the book you're writing, and you've got to write about what you want to become. So I knew this topic would force me to take a deep dive into the principles of great health and straight into creating it for myself and my family. Today, that's where I find myself. I'm under 210 pounds, which is the least I've weighed in over twenty years. It feels amazing!

My confidence and energy are through the roof, and it's more about how I feel than how I look. Self-confidence comes from keeping your own commitments to yourself. When you let yourself down with poor financial or health decisions, you hurt your confidence in yourself. That security doesn't come from the outside but from within.

The more you keep your commitments to yourself regarding your health, the more confident you feel, the more energy you have, the more capacity you have to work, and the more impact you can make on the world. It's exactly as Dan Sullivan said it in the foreword of this book!

I am the designer of my destiny. I am the author of my autobiography. And so are you. *You* write the story of your life. Nobody can write your financial story, and nobody can write your health and energy story. The pen is, and always will be, in your hand.

Why not write a story that is exciting and limitless? In this book, I'll show you seven principles to do just that:

1. Be ridiculously ambitious
2. Avoid temptations
3. Hire only top experts
4. Transform with technology
5. Leverage the compound effect
6. Cut the excuses
7. Fortify your legacy

Let's get started.

"If your dreams don't scare you, they are too small."

– RICHARD BRANSON

1

BE RIDICULOUSLY
AMBITIOUS

My friend and client Keegan Caldwell struggled all his years in middle and high school and began serving in the U.S. military as a teenager. He was wrapping up his service in his early twenties and was supposed to arrive home on September 13, 2001.

Then, 9/11 happened.

The military said, essentially, "Never mind, you're not going home anymore." They sent him to Iraq and Afghanistan, where he was in the thick of it, risking his life. He came home with PTSD and all kinds of injuries. Through his treatments and recovery, he became addicted to pain medication, which led to harder drugs, and cycled in and out of rehab centers. He didn't have much support, and nothing was sticking.

The story could have ended there, but thankfully, it didn't.

He decided to be ridiculously ambitious and set a goal to get himself cleaned up and attempt to go get a college degree.

The goal seemed impossible, but he did a complete 180. He received his undergraduate diploma, followed by a PhD! Then he decided to take the bar exam without going to law school. Almost no one can pass the bar without two or three years of law school, but technically you're allowed to. Even making the attempt was ridiculously ambitious, let alone putting in the sufficient study work to succeed. He passed, became an intellectual patent attorney, and then started his own law firm, which became the fastest-growing firm in the United States in 2022 (Inc. Magazine).[1] He's now focused on building one of the first $100-million-a-year law firms in his niche category.

In short, Keegan went from a struggling high school student to a veteran struggling with addiction and PTSD to being an incredibly successful entrepreneur, with thriving law office hubs in Los Angeles, Boston, and London. He's been featured all over in big media publications, getting the due credit for how hard he's worked.[2] He now employs a large number of people, many of whom come from similarly tough backgrounds. He's helping pass on his success through his ridiculous ambition, and he just keeps going, without being held back by fear.

Back in his days in Iraq, Keegan was a machine gunner on top of a tank carrying out many missions in the middle of the night, a role in which he learned hesitation and fear lead to your death. He had to go full force into missions without second-guessing himself or the goal, and he now takes that same approach to his business and his health

> "I'm sure you can imagine that as a sixth time convicted felon that many people told me that I would never be able to accomplish this. In fact, one of those people was my very first attorney on one of my cases. I'd had too much to drink one night, things got out of hand, and I tore this bar apart. I was charged with malicious destruction of property, a felony in Michigan. I know it was a product of the pattern of substance abuse I'd had before and that some of my behavior spilled over from my time in the Marine Corps. But still, I wanted to know what my options were and what this meant for the rest of my life.
>
> I asked my lawyer if I'd ever be able to become an attorney down the road if I was convicted of a crime—which I was. He said 'no' and I took that to heart. In fact, I think a lot of career options are not available for people who are in positions like mine.
>
> However, I did my diligence and poked around on the internet. I researched in the Public Law Library to see what rules and ethical guidelines existed for someone to become an attorney. Each state has its own rules, but all in all, it seemed there might be a path forward for me! But I decided to go ahead and get my undergrad degree after I got sober. After finishing my undergrad degree, I went on to get a PhD in physical

chemistry. From there, I actually took the Patent Bar Exam and the State Bar exam without having gone to law school... and here I am today."

— KEEGAN CALDWELL // FOUNDER OF
CALDWELL IP

He's not a runner by nature, but he set himself a goal to run a 5k. Though it was hard, he did it. Then, he did it again the next day. And the next day. And the next day—for 380 consecutive days—rain, shine, travel, snow. No matter the circumstances, he showed up for his goal.

He flew to Chicago one time, arriving after midnight, and he hadn't run yet because he'd been in meetings all day. He ran in the middle of the cold, dark night. Another time, he was sick as a dog and skipped all his meetings at a conference, but he got out of his hotel bed, coughing and wheezing, and went for a run in the freezing rain before getting back in bed to keep his consistency streak alive. You can probably tell that Keegan is next-level and absolutely epitomizes facing discomfort and pain, which is inherent to your journey of growth. There's a Buddhist saying that states pain is inevitable, but suffering is optional. You've probably heard that pain is weakness leaving the body, and he doesn't seem to have any weakness left.

Keegan is a speaker and mentor for AA and has been sober for a decade now. He still goes to weekly meetings, and he mentors and counsels people who are struggling with addiction. Having achieved success, he remains invested in the well-being of others, volunteering in the community to help people with struggles like his. If that's not a legacy move, I don't know what is.

Dan Sullivan says all progress starts by telling the truth. You have to face the facts, which include uncomfortable realities and necessary confrontations, whether that's addiction, overspending, debt, excess weight, or a health condition. Set your sights ridiculously high and then do what you need to do to break through, because on the other side of discomfort and fear is success.

The late basketball legend Kobe Bryant (known as "the Black Mamba") once said, "One of the main takeaways was that you have to work hard in the dark to shine in the light. Meaning: It takes a lot of work to be successful. A lot of people say they want to be great, but they're not willing to make the sacrifices necessary to achieve greatness. They have other concerns, whether important or not, and they spread themselves out. That's totally fine. After all, greatness is not for everybody."

If you want to be elite, there's no shortcut: you're going to have to put in the work. This is the frame of mind you need to tackle this book and implement what I'm teaching. If you're not ready to do that, close this book and pick it back up when you are.

SO... WHAT IS RIDICULOUS AMBITION?

We limit ourselves by assessing our potential based only on our current capabilities, our current circumstances, our current reach, and our current understanding and expertise. Too often, people fail to give themselves permission to think beyond where they currently are. **However, in my experience, those who achieve incredible goals are those who refuse to accept the limitations of their current circumstances.** There are no excuses in today's day and age to not create great wealth and great health. You can try to debate me on that, but we'll forever disagree. And I believe people who are highly successful know the truth.

If you want to talk about ridiculous ambition, let me tell you about my wife, Amber. She's a prime example of this. With some encouragement from a few of our friends, Amber decided on New Year's Day that she wanted to train for and compete in a half-Ironman: that's a 1.2-mile swim, fifty-six-mile bike ride, and 13.1-mile run, back-to-back-to-back. She'd never ran more than five miles in a row in her life and didn't even own a bike, but none of that stopped her.

An active and amazing mother of five, and beyond her thirties, she committed to this new goal and made the time to train between two and four hours a day, borrowing an older, used bike from a friend. I vividly remember arriving at our hotel late at night in Costa Rica after a long day of travel, and she got her cap and goggles and went straight to the pool to swim laps for an hour.

There were so many times where she could've made excuses and skipped her training, but she kept fighting and pushing herself forward. When the race came four months later in May, she not only finished the race, she finished twenty-ninth in her age bracket. What seemed like an impossible goal (getting ready for a half-Ironman in less than five months) at first was achieved in a very short amount of time. Shockingly, though her body was tired and exhausted the next day, she woke up determined to race again and improve her time. She's now preparing for two more Ironman races that are coming up very soon. Amber inspires me to be disciplined and push my limits every day. When you have that mindset, there simply are no good excuses.

In my primary business (Pacific Capital), I work with many successful entrepreneurs, lots of "Type A personalities." They're all doing exceptionally well in the wealth department, but have a hard time acknowledging it. They get caught up in comparing themselves to others who have more than them. The point about being ridiculously ambitious, though, is not about focusing on what you lack. It's actually about not accepting your current situation as your ceiling. If you think you're doing great, that doesn't mean you can't do greater.

Ask yourself: What would happen if this year you actually kept all of your commitments to yourself, everything you say you want to do? How different would your life be just a year from now?

> "The reasonable man adapts himself to the world: the unreasonable one persists in trying to adapt the world to himself. Therefore, all progress depends on the unreasonable man."
>
> — GEORGE BERNARD SHAW

Personally, I just don't get motivated by small goals. They don't excite me at all. Small and "realistic" goals don't get me off the couch to do anything. But on the other hand, something exciting, challenging, and seemingly impossible sparks a ton of energy and gets my brain activated. I actually love transformational goals and ideas. I find myself thinking: *It seems impossible, but what if it wasn't? What if I could actually make this idea a reality? How would that feel?*

That exact feeling motivated me to kick off my weight loss journey that I shared in the Intro. At first, when I got home from Denver, I started making changes and getting in better shape on my own. I lost a noticeable amount of weight in the first few weeks by just eating less and eating healthier, but I was still searching and lacking coaching support that I knew was needed for me to reach the next level. No way could I lose fifty pounds without any help. And I didn't want to make yet another great burst of progress in my health and fitness, and then fall back down to where I started. My new resolution and determination launched me forward, but it was time to get some help and expertise to keep it going. I wrote down my goals and made my commitments public. To add a degree of accountability, I told my close friends and family about my personal goals.

Then I started looking for a fitness expert. I've had personal trainers before, but no system or coach to this point had helped me achieve the results I wanted. So one night I noticed my good friend Jonny posting on Instagram, and noticed something very different: he looked younger, fitter, and stronger than he had in probably twenty years. We met in college as freshmen living in the dorms, but haven't lived in the same state since graduating over twenty years ago. I did what any good friend would do, and gave him some compliments and recognition in the comments on his post, and then sent him a DM to ask what his secret was! It turns out he'd joined an intense fitness coaching program for high-level entrepreneurs and CEOs. After some research and exploratory calls with that company, I decided to give it a shot myself.

When I talked to the trainer, Ryan, for the first time, he asked me to tell him about my health and physical fitness goals. I told him I wanted to lose forty-five to fifty pounds. He said, "Wow, Great! That's a lot to lose in a year."

"No," I said, "I want to lose that in three months."

He gasped on the Zoom call. Then, he basically told me that was a bit insane, maybe not even possible. Of course, Ryan was polite about it and didn't want to discourage his new excited client from going for it.

I explained to him that I wouldn't be inspired to take massive action unless the goal seemed impossible. That's just how I'm wired. Maybe you can relate? **When you set a target that truly challenges and inspires you, the fun part is not even reaching the goal per se—it's seeing who you become in the process.**

As it turned out, I didn't quite reach my ambitious three-month goal. I fell short. But I came pretty close: I lost forty-three pounds in three months. No gimmicks, no pills, no surgeries or fad diet programs. And through this process, I've cemented new habits and completely changed my lifestyle. Because of these changes, I feel energetic and better every day, which impacts every other area of my life. By setting an ambitious target rather than an easy one, I was forced to face the truth and make drastic changes (in what I ate, how much I ate, how much water I drank, how many hours I slept, how I worked out, etc.). I tell you this story because I just went through all of this personally and feel there are great take-away lessons we can learn from my short journey. To transform your life and reach ambitious goals, you're forced to modify your existing habits for the better and stop the excuses that have held you back. Because you're aiming for a nearly impossible goal, you become a new person. It's the only option to get there. The same transformation doesn't happen when you set small, incremental goals.

If you want an example of ridiculous ambition, look no further than "The Iron Cowboy"—James Lawrence.

For many years, the world record for completing full Ironman races was twenty in one year. James decided to not just challenge that record and go for twenty-one, but to do something ridiculous. He took on the challenge of doing fifty long-distance triathlons in fifty consecutive days through all fifty U.S. states! That's 2.4 miles of swimming, 112 miles of cycling and a full 26.2-mile marathon run every day for fifty days straight, while traveling in a motorhome between most states and barely getting four hours of sleep each night. He was told it wasn't possible and was "repeatedly mocked for choosing a goal so big." But guess what? He did it. But he didn't stop there. "I felt like I had some unfinished business with the fifty [iron-distance triathlons in fifty days in fifty states]," said Lawrence. "When the pandemic hit in 2020, I went from eighty speaking events a year to zero. I took this as an opportunity for me to have time to train for one last wild tear—so I went for it: 101 iron-distance triathlons in 101 days." He did this in 2021, the year he turned forty-five years old, beginning on a freezing cold day in March with snow-covered mountains all around him. James is perhaps the most ridiculously ambitious person I've ever met.

Most people are living in their own version of *Groundhog Day* or *The Truman Show*, just repeating their same habit cycle over and over again. They go to the same coffee shop, drop their kids off at school, make the same commute to work, come home, eat the same thing, watch the same show, and scroll through social media, only to wake up and do it all over again. How boring and miserable!

Why not mix it up? If you're a growth-focused entrepreneur, you know you probably seek a lot of new variety and challenges that make you rise to your full potential. Extreme financial success can lead to complacency. It might be tempting for you to shift from a high gear into neutral and just coast to the finish line. If you're reading this book and you're the kind of person I believe you are, you like to stir up change, you actually seek the stress that new challenges bring. For example, instead of just keeping the status quo in your business, you get the crazy idea to grow 10X in four years, and that big target lights a new fire under you. You actually have fun trying to figure out how to make those big goals and dreams a reality.

I've done this professionally, too—not just with my health. When I was just thirty-two years old, I had the big corner office and worked in a very prominent spotlight at Merrill Lynch. Out of seventeen thousand advisors, I was in the top two percent of the company nationally. But I didn't feel challenged anymore. The people and big Wall Street bureaucracy around me felt very stale and hollow. So, like the movie character Jerry McGuire (played by actor Tom Cruise), I packed up my boxes one day and just walked out, bringing just my assistant with me. I gave up a very comfortable seven-figure income to completely start over from scratch with nothing but bills, expenses, payroll, and lease payments—and no assurance of any kind of success in the future. I didn't have a single client, because legal compliance in our industry prevented me from speaking to any clients before making the move. Talk about taking a leap of faith and disrupting a comfortable status quo!

I'd never been an entrepreneur before, so this was completely unknown territory. Thankfully, we've built something many times more significant than what the business I built while at Merrill Lynch. In the land of unconstrained independence, we've grown Pacific Capital to be one of the top fiduciary family offices in the country and have a team of professional experts who are totally aligned with my big goals and vision. They're on board for the excitement and challenges of being part of an entrepreneurial firm that sets ridiculously ambitious goals. Forget the numbers themselves, the journey itself has been extremely rewarding.

My friend and client Casey Adams is another excellent example of ridiculous ambition when it comes to wealth building and achieving big goals. He left his career as a lawyer to become an entrepreneur, buying a transportation and logistics company that he grew and eventually sold to a global public company for $800 million in less than six years.

Casey was named Ernst & Young Entrepreneur of the Year in the state of Utah for his great accomplishments. He saw an opportunity to take what he'd learned in the corporate world and apply his leadership skills, management techniques, deal-making ability, and relationship-building to chart his own path, which paid off exponentially. A savvy business decision-maker, he now serves on many boards and advises CEOs and founders—all because they've seen what Casey's leadership and ambition can produce.

When you set a ridiculous goal, it's not so much about a specific endpoint or final milestone as it is about the process and growth that the uphill climb requires—the transformation it makes inside of you and the world. If you're trying to make $10 million by a specific year to feed one million kids in an impoverished country and you "only" feed 950,000 by your target date, you've still changed the world in a way you would not have if you'd tried to make a one-time donation to help one kid. The point is to aim so high you're forced to strive far beyond what you think is possible. As you achieve bigger and better things, who you are becomes bigger and better, too. You stretch in service of the goal until you become a new person. It's the difference between exponential and linear growth, and it's always within your reach if you adopt the right mindset.

> *"In tenth grade, I went to my first summer conditioning practice for the high school football team and got completely embarrassed. I was the scrawniest and weakest kid on the team and was so insecure about*

my strength and body. I had two choices: never return to the weight room again or run straight into my insecurity. I quit the football team and became obsessed with improving my body. This passion led me all the way to the National Football League, where I lived a childhood dream despite never playing a single down of high school football. Most people run away from insecurities; I run straight into them and make them strengths."

— JOHN MADSEN // CEO OF SUPRA HUMAN

CONFRONTING PROBLEMS AND EXCUSES RIGHT AWAY

Maybe you look around and think you're already doing pretty well and don't have any reasons to change or improve. There could be areas of your health and wealth you could work on, sure, but you've decided that you're doing "good enough." But what kind of way to live is that? You only get one life. And life is not graded on a curve.

A guiding quote in my life is actually one that defines hell as when "your last day on earth, the person you became will meet the person you could have become." That gap is hellish because it represents your untapped potential. Most of us only use a tiny fraction of our potential. What could your life look like if you leveraged more of it? Why not start today and find out?

Being ridiculously ambitious plays to the inherent strengths of an entrepreneur. If you're reading this book, I'll bet you have those strengths and have reached a certain level of success that sets you apart. You're already ridiculously ambitious for even reading this type of book. If you've gotten to this point, I know who you are. You're the 0.01 percent who has insane goals and who wants a lifestyle that most people don't even care to think about. Beyond liking a post or sharing a picture on social media, you are actually seeking ways to create the life you imagine.

This isn't a "but" situation—it's an "and" situation. You are already wildly successful, *and* it doesn't make sense to limit yourself. You can be financially successful *and* have amazing health; it doesn't make sense to choose one over the other. If you only have one of the two, you're not maximizing your full potential. How can you remove the artificial ceiling on what's possible for you?

 "Breaking through our own barriers often means dealing with naysayers, and I've experienced this time and time again in my life. Almost every major leap forward I've made has been met with skepticism and doubt. I've been called crazy, unreasonable, and insane, but I've learned that unreasonable growth demands transformational commitments that others might not grasp.

Take, for example, the time I purchased a 60,000-square-foot, $20 million building during the peak of COVID-19 in March 2020. People thought I'd lost my mind, but I saw the opportunity and seized it. That decision turned out to be one of the best I've ever made and expanded the capabilities of our organization tenfold.

And when I chose to invest $8 million in hosting a massive conference (The Crisp Game Changers Summit) for over five thousand growth-minded attorneys at the Mercedes-Benz Stadium, the naysayers were convinced I'd embarrass myself. But I knew better, and that event ended up being the largest conference in the history of the legal industry and a tremendous success.

So, how did I handle the doubters? I remained laser-focused on my vision, refusing to be swayed by the opinions of those who couldn't see the potential for greatness. I recognized that being called unreasonable or insane was actually a sign that I was pushing boundaries and refusing to settle for mediocrity.

The bottom line is this: as you shatter your own limits, there will always be people who question your decisions and doubt your capabilities.

Stay true to your vision, trust your gut, and surround yourself with individuals who share your relentless drive for growth and success. In the end, it's not about proving them wrong—it's about proving to yourself that you have the power to overcome any obstacle and achieve greatness."

— MICHAEL MOGILL // FOUNDER & CEO OF
CRISP

Over the following chapters, I'll help you take action, make progress, and see the possibilities and correlations of creating a lifestyle beyond your wildest dreams. If you're reading this book, you believe that creating both incredible health and significant legacy family wealth is possible. Both matter to you. Why? What's inside you that makes these two topics so important to you? Is it your family, your legacy, your lifestyle opportunities, your freedom? The biggest reason people become entrepreneurs is for freedom. I've said it many times before: financial freedom is less about finances and more about freedom.

Freedom from addiction—combined with incredible energy, physical and mental health, and significant financial wealth —is the ultimate freedom. If you're trapped in bad habits, addictions, debt, and other choices that undermine your financial life, then you're constrained and restricted from being who you were meant to be. Tapping into your desire for peak experiences and a lifestyle of freedom will drive you to pursue the paths of health and wealth simultaneously. It's no coincidence that Pacific Capital's value proposition is increasing lifestyle and financial freedom for eight and nine-figure entrepreneurs. I believe in this power so much that I built my entire company in service of it.

As I discussed in my first book, *Stress-Free Money*, such freedom leads to less stress. Stress has negative effects on both physical health and financial wealth, and stress from one area impacts the other. The more you can free yourself from its effects, the more you can continue to push the limits of achievement and enjoyment, cultivating a feedback loop of confidence and success in both health and wealth. **In short, attending to your health is beneficial to your wealth, and vice versa.**

In the context of being ridiculously ambitious, sometimes you need to aim higher than you first thought. There's inherent risk in that stance, but there's a difference between stress that weighs you down and adrenaline backed by confidence in your abilities. Nervousness and excitement have similar physical signs, but they come from fundamentally different places.

You can't live entirely without stress, so focus instead on putting healthy stress on yourself in the form of challenging yourself to grow and become better. Exercise puts healthy stress on your body and mind. Over time, your workouts create energy and momentum.

Any ridiculously ambitious goal toward prosperity does the same—you build your own momentum. Rockets burn most of their fuel at takeoff; after that, they can use their momentum to coast. It's much easier to fly after liftoff and takes less energy once you've fully launched. Choose the right goals to fully launch yourself, and you'll find you can more easily continue on the right path.

> *"Don't limit yourself. Many people limit themselves to what they think they can do. You can go as far as your mind lets you. What you believe, you can achieve."*

— MARY KAY ASH

As Dan Sullivan wrote about in his book *Wanting What You Want*, you don't have to justify your desires or goals... whether they're related to health, wealth, or a bucket list of experiences. You can do whatever the heck you want. Give yourself permission to go after goals and experiences that would be fulfilling, meaningful, and significant to you and your family.

Do you remember those crabs in the bucket I mentioned earlier in this book? **There will always be some people around you who will try to pull you down to their level. This is even more true when you set ridiculously ambitious goals because most of the people around you will not relate to you.** They might think you're selfish, arrogant, or trying to separate yourself from them, but usually they're projecting their own feelings of disappointment in having let *themselves* down. If they haven't achieved what they want, then they don't want to see anyone else surpass them because it stirs up those bad feelings.

What does this mean for you? Tune out the people who are less ambitious or don't have your best interests at heart. Sometimes those people are even friends or members of your family. They might not see the potential of your dream or why you want what you want. They might tell you to relax and just be happy with what you have.

When I left Merrill Lynch, people in my inner circle questioned my decision. Why wasn't I just staying where I was comfortable and already doing so well? In theory, they weren't trying to undermine me—they wanted what was best for me. But they couldn't see the bigger picture.

Most people seek comfort over potential. It's too much of a risk for them to acknowledge what's possible when they haven't done it themselves. They fail to look at possibility head-on and instead stay in their comfort zone. **But there's no growth in the comfort zone. Growth comes from aiming to break through limits.**

Fast track your success by the number of uncomfortable conversations you're having. As an entrepreneur, the level of success you achieve is often dependent upon the number of uncomfortable conversations you embrace. If you avoid the hard talks with employees, clients, your spouse, your doctor, or yourself, you'll never move past the obstacles. You can't overcome what you avoid. Facing discomfort is required for major growth.

> *"I tend to challenge myself physically and mentally with epic birthday workouts, such as running twenty miles on my twentieth birthday, swimming three thousand meters consecutively on my thirtieth birthday, doing thirty-five unbroken pull-ups for my*

thirty-fifth birthday, etc. Last year, I set what I would consider to be a ridiculously ambitious goal for my fortieth birthday... and learned that sometimes setting the bar too high can result in 'biting off more than you can chew' and ultimately failure, disappointment, and potentially public embarrassment if you (like me) tend to share your goals publicly on locations such as social media. In this case, for my fortieth birthday, I set a goal of a four-minute breath hold on the exhale, a 40kg Turkish get-up with the kettlebell for each side of my body, a 4000m swim, and a 400m run in one minute and ten seconds.

The lofty goal not only resulted in failure, but also a string of injuries I didn't live down until nearly my forty-first birthday. Long story short: set lofty goals (and I recommend birthdays for this!) but don't make them so ambitious that while they look good in your dreams, they just don't make sense in terms of your physical or time limitations!"

— BEN GREENFIELD // CEO & FOUNDER OF
BEN GREENFIELD LIFE, CO-FOUNDER
OF KION

ALL IN

I've always been driven by action. If I'm going to do something, I give it everything.

In fact, I hesitate to commit to some things because I know once I do so, I'll go all in. Before I say yes to a project or opportunity, it's important to me to ensure I can give it everything I've got. It's not an option for me to go halfway. If I agree to host an event, I need to confirm I've got the time and capacity because I won't put on something mediocre. I'll make it the best, most memorable experience I can, which takes a significant amount of energy and teamwork. That's just my personality.

When you're fully invested in everything that you do, you have to accept an inherent level of risk because you publicly own the outcome, good or bad. I'm a huge fan of Michael Jordan and the late Kobe Bryant, for example, who were always willing to take the last, game-winning shot, knowing that if they missed, the blame would be on them. Michael Jordan famously said, "Twenty-six times, I've been trusted to take the game-winning shot and missed. I've failed over and over and over again in my life. And that is why I succeed." **People who are ridiculously ambitious seek out that degree of pressure because it challenges them to grow and to step up in the big moments.**

You've already taken those risks in life and in business, and now we can talk about new ways to keep leveling up. A good place to start is to tackle the well-known SMART goal framework, with a twist:

SPECIFIC

MEASURABLE

ACHIEVABLE

~~REALISTIC~~ RIDICULOUS

TIME-BOUND

Specificity is a great framework, but don't set a limit for yourself with realism. REALISTIC goals are boring and they won't transform your life. Change the **R** to RIDICULOUS.

If you set a ridiculous goal for your health, the progress you make and the change in who you are can fuel you to pursue a ridiculous goal for your wealth. The momentum keeps going, and the two areas feed off each other.

You set—or break through—your own ceiling. Keep raising your personal ceiling by keeping your commitments to yourself. The byproduct will be the ability to do more for not only yourself but also for others, expanding your impact.

 "Your only limit is the amount of action you take."

— JACK CANFIELD

SO MUCH TO GAIN

Setting ambitious goals requires you to step out of your comfort zone and challenge yourself. When you achieve these goals, you gain a sense of accomplishment and confidence in your abilities, which then leads to momentum for more achievement.

Confidence comes simply from keeping your commitments to yourself; it's a measure of how strong your reputation is with yourself. If you keep your own commitments and are who you say you are, you'll have plenty of confidence.

Ridiculous ambition also creates a sense of purpose. Having a big, audacious goal gives you a clear direction and focus in life. When you have something to strive for, you wake up each day with a sense of purpose and motivation.

It drives innovation: when you set ambitious goals, you're forced to think creatively and come up with innovative solutions. This can lead to new discoveries and breakthroughs that can change your life... and maybe even change the world.

> *"My biggest naysayer has always been myself. The voice in my head that got in young, constantly criticizing me and reminding me why I'm not good enough. The more I've grown, the more I've been able to recognize the voice, call it out, and stop it in its tracks. I call it 'firewalling' thoughts, just like you would a virus on a computer. Knowing 'yeah, this is*

mine, but it didn't come from me. It came from years of unhappiness and suffering from previous generations in my family, and was passed down to me.' In many homes, this is how children are talked to: they're looked down upon, shamed, and that's sadly the self-limiting programming they inherit. But understand it's simply how the parents were raised, and it's also how they talk to themselves. With a little discipline and a lot of faith, you can begin to break those generational curses and talk to yourself like the parent you never had. That's what I'm committed to working on now, and it's had immense positive ripple effects across my life and my business.

In fact, in 2020 I had a goal of making $1 million a month. It was the first time in my life I was running my own company, my blog really took off, and money started to come at me fast. I was suddenly hitting $100,000 months consistently and got wide eyes for more. I hired coaches, more team members, and attempted to wish the money into existence, but never really did the disciplined work of building a sustainable, scalable offer, or facing the unavoidable hard work it takes to really get there. That was three years ago now and my revenue has not yet grown, but God instead took me on a beautiful path of dismantling my ego, and my entitlement, which would not have served the world well had it gone on any longer. After all, no one likes inflated egos, and more money just makes that worse. It was definitely *painful to have years go by and not make more money like I had hoped, but I see now why it didn't happen. I am learning to let go of the 'need', the impatience, the gluttony, and instead practice faith that the universe is always arranging itself in my favor. I feel I'm finally on the right track of becoming a more worthy person, a more heart-centered business owner, before God brings more riches my way. My mindset has shifted completely and today, I am just grateful for the money I do have, and I trust the rest is on its way."*

— SHAY ROWBOTTOM // MARKETING
ENTREPRENEUR & SOCIAL MEDIA
INFLUENCER

INSPIRING OTHERS

One of my favorite books is *The Energy Bus* by Jon Gordon. It's an allegory about a bus ride, demonstrating how contagious energy is. I've had everyone at the company read it and think about what kind of energy they bring to our team. When you cultivate your own energy and surround yourself with energizing people, the collective motivation will keep everyone sharp and growing.

Change is not just about yourself. It's also about leading by example and being a positive influence in the lives of the people you love.

Ridiculous ambition inspires others. When you pursue ambitious goals, you inspire others to do the same. Your actions and achievements motivate others to reach for their own dreams and aspirations.

It's important to bring your family and social connections into the conversation about ambition, so you're not just high-achieving at work but then exhausted or checked out at home. Infusing this value into everything I do, in every area of my life, is at the core of who I am striving to be.

With any goal, financial or otherwise, climbing to the mountaintop is only fun when you're doing it with those you care about. High achievement and success are not reserved just for me. They're not part of a zero-sum game in which my success prevents someone else from having that chance. *Everyone* can be successful.

On LinkedIn, I spend time encouraging other financial advisors and giving them tips and advice, instead of thinking of them as competitors and hoarding my knowledge and experience to myself. I genuinely wish them success. I feel zero competitive spirit with people in my industry. There's absolutely enough to go around. Too often, people believe they have to do well at the expense of others, but it's simply not true.

If everyone thrives, succeeds, and helps each other, there will be even greater opportunities for all of us. We can lift each other up instead of pulling each other back down. So why wouldn't I encourage people around me to reach for big goals?

I also want my family to learn from what I've learned. I've spent years in deep study on self-improvement goals, life planning, financial success, and entrepreneurship. More than money, I want to pass down that knowledge so they can benefit from the mindsets and wisdom I've gained through my struggles and studies. Bringing the energy of ambitious goals and achievement to my family and my inner circle is key.

When it comes to success, growth compounds even more rapidly when you include your inner circle. There's a larger ripple effect when people are on the same page instead of acting as individuals.

In short, unified teams win. Team chemistry matters. Imagine a team with one superstar trying to lift up the other players. Now imagine a team composed entirely of unified, motivated superstars working in alignment. The latter team will win championships, thrive, and elevate each other to new heights. A great example of a sports team that achieved success due to their unity is the 2004 Detroit Pistons in the NBA. The 2004 Pistons, led by Coach Larry Brown, lacked a superstar in the traditional sense but relied heavily on team-work, unity, and collective defense. Their roster included players like Chauncey Billups, Ben Wallace, Rasheed Wallace, Richard Hamilton, and Tayshaun Prince. What they lacked in individual superstar power, they made up for in cohesion, defensive tenacity, and shared responsibility on the offensive end.

In the 2004 NBA Finals, they faced the Los Angeles Lakers, a team stacked with hall-of-famers like Shaquille O'Neal, Kobe Bryant, Karl Malone, and Gary Payton. Despite the Lakers being heavy favorites, the Pistons won the series 4–1, with a team-first approach that highlighted their unity and cohesion. As a longtime Laker season ticket holder, this example is burned into my memories, and it still hurts a bit. The victory was widely recognized as a triumph of teamwork and unity over individual star power.

I believe we can all relate to the desire of being surrounded by people who are motivating and energizing each other towards greatness. I don't want to be the one successful person carrying everyone else's weight all the time. Sometimes we all need an extra push and encouragement, including me. If my family has cultivated an ambitious commitment to success, then I can encourage them when they need it, and they can encourage me. My wife and kids notice when I need a boost to lift me to my full potential, and I'm grateful we can help each other. It's a symbiotic relationship.

My family loves basketball; as of this writing, our oldest daughter McKinley is a freshman basketball player at Brigham Young University, playing in the BIG 12 Conference.

Our kids all play basketball, and some play volleyball and football too. My wife and I have sat on the bleachers to watch thousands of games, matches, and practices at gyms and fields all across the country. When I think about a team of unified superstars playing together, I want to emulate that same dynamic in our home. **Inevitably, you and everyone around you will overcome challenging circumstances more frequently, quickly, and successfully if everyone has a mindset of success and achievement than if you are the only one that everyone depends on. I want everyone around me to have energy to give as well. Like a big**

potluck dinner party on Thanksgiving, it's better when everyone shows up with their best contribution to the feast.

> "Our most valuable resource is time. Thus, allocating as much of my time to my 'highest and best use' (based upon my why) is the key to having a bigger impact. Yet we all have certain 'requirements' for stewarding our lives that tend to stand in the way of devoting maximum time to our why.
>
> In my experience, those who have the biggest impact are those who are the most effective at simplifying what they can, outsourcing the remaining essentials to the degree possible, and reallocating that recaptured time toward their why."
>
> — MATT MUNSON // FOUNDER OF SERVANT FINANCIAL LLC

Being ridiculously ambitious leads to a more fulfilling, purposeful, and successful life. I encourage my wife, my five kids, my extended family, my clients, my friends, and my readers, including you, to dream big and strive for greatness.

Try these tips:

• Challenge yourself to have uncomfortable but necessary conversations–starting with yourself.

  – Have the uncomfortable conversation with yourself in the mirror about what's holding you back. What do you keep telling yourself is 'too impossible?'

  – Avoid common excuses like "I don't have time to exercise" or "There's a lot of economic uncertainty, so it's not a great time to invest."

• Involve others in your plans and go all-in.

  – Have a health and fitness challenge with friends, family, or colleagues.

  – Join or create groups of people who are striving to increase their wealth.

• Set specific goals that are sticky, ridiculous, and drive the kind of massive transformation that leads to success.

  – Read or listen to *10X is Easier than 2X* by Dan Sullivan and Dr. Benjamin Hardy. Think about what 10X goals seem impossible to you in your own life.

  – Write down one 10X goal for your own life.

> **EXAMPLES OF RIDICULOUS GOALS**
>
> *HEALTH:* "I am going to have no alcohol, candy, dessert, or treats for one year."
>
> *HEALTH:* "I want to become medication-free and pain-free in less than one year."
>
> *WEALTH:* "I want my investments to create passive income from seven different sources, with each source providing enough to cover my lifestyle expenses."
>
> *WEALTH:* "I want to take one luxury lifestyle vacation a month."

  – Reflect on three things you've accomplished or experienced that seemed out of reach 10–15 years ago. This will help you recognize that it is possible.

  – Find three people who inspire you because of the incredible things they've accomplished. If you have access to them, ask them about their experiences directly. If you don't, become a student of their journey.

"The greatest victory is the battle not fought."

– SUN TZU

2

AVOID TEMPTATIONS

When I was fifteen years old, my mom sat me down for a serious talk. She said, "There are certain indulgences and harmful things that people really like, which later in life become addictions that cause a lot of grief and sorrow." She told me about her friends who'd had a hard time quitting the bad habits they'd picked up. The easiest way to avoid that struggle, she advised, was to never start.

She continued, "There should be a few things in your life that someday you can tell your kids, 'I've never _____.'" She wasn't talking about obvious things *no one* should do, like committing a felony, but rather choices I could make as a young person that would help my future self. People make mistakes in high school and college that often impact their life trajectory into their fifties and sixties.

For example, my mom told me she'd never drunk alcohol or smoked. She'd simply decided not to, because she saw no possible positive impact from them. So she never even tried them in the first place. As a teenager, I looked up to my mom and we were very close friends, and I thought what she was describing sounded like a cool challenge.

To this day, I can honestly say I've never had a sip of alcohol and never smoked. I was often invited to parties where I knew there would be peer pressure and activities beyond even smoking and drinking, and avoided the temptation by simply declining the invite and not putting myself in that environment.

Temptation is the universe's way of testing your commitment to your dreams and goals. If you want to be successful, you have to learn to say no to the things that distract you from your goals.

> *"Temptation is the feeling that you are the most important person in the world, and that your desires should be fulfilled at any cost."*

> — UNKNOWN

IDENTIFYING YOUR TEMPTATIONS

I was recently at a dinner in Florida, which included very expensive bottles of wine. Out of fourteen people at our table, three of us decided not to have the wine. Someone then commented, "I've never seen Chad drink."

"That's because I never have," I replied.

"Wait, never?"

"Nope, not once." It shocked them, but it's the truth.

Please don't misinterpret this at all. I don't judge people who drink alcohol; I made a commitment to myself as a kid, and I've never gone back on that commitment. There aren't too many people who can say the same. It doesn't make me better than anyone, but it's an internal marker of keeping a commitment over a very long time period, which I believe demonstrates credibility and integrity.

Odds are your trajectory looks different. Have you gotten involved in any habits that don't serve your goals? That's okay. **Even if you're not starting from a clean slate, that doesn't mean you can't avoid temptation moving forward.** Find out what temptation looks like for you, and then set yourself up to avoid it strategically.

How? Simple: start by identifying one temptation that has negatively impacted your health or wealth building, and then pick a date (sooner, not later) when you'll start new, fresh, and clean to make better decisions moving forward. You get to break the chain of addiction or bad habits.

If you're off track now, forgive yourself, move on and keep moving forward. Avoiding temptation is not always easy, and you may slip up. If you do, forgive yourself and get back on track. Don't let a moment of weakness hold you back from achieving your goals. Aim to bounce back quickly and stay committed for the long haul.

A friend of mine had been making incredible gains in his physical fitness but told me he "fell off the wagon" during the holidays last year. He was feeling so low about falling off the wagon that he'd decided, through inaction, to stay off the wagon.

I reminded him of how far he'd come in the previous two years and reassured him that a couple months of losing his way didn't negate his potential and progress. If you step back and look at where he is today compared to the previous ten years, he's still in a great spot, so I encouraged him to pick himself back up. **The best way to avoid temptation is never to start, but there are always areas where we need to course-correct, no matter how careful we are. Don't get so stuck in all-or-nothing mindsets that you decide your situation is beyond fixing.**

This perspective connects to the book *The Gap and the Gain* by Dr. Benjamin Hardy and Dan Sullivan. Comparing yourself to ideal expectations that are unrealistic to your circumstances puts you in the gap. Instead, focus on the progress you've already made and the self-awareness you already have—the gain. Pick a date, start over, and remove the temptations that cause you to make bad financial decisions, like credit card spending, big impulse purchases, and uninformed or foolish investments.

For example, many of my clients have a tendency to get excited about new business opportunities they hear about at parties or conferences and they invest a few hundred thousand dollars because they're intrigued by the person or the story. That's a temptation.

Ideally, as part of their strategy to avoid that temptation, my clients should come talk to our team about their plans and ideas they heard before committing to invest a large chunk of money. My approach will always be to dig into the actual details beyond the compelling pitch and the fear of missing out.

 "Avoiding temptation is easier when you know what you stand to lose."

— UNKNOWN

In choosing this commitment (to be completely non-alcoholic) that goes against the American mainstream, I haven't experienced a fear of missing out. Why? It's easier to be one hundred percent committed than ninety-eight percent committed, as Dr. Ben Hardy famously teaches.[1]

Swimmer Michael Phelps is an amazing example of commitment and dedication. He spent over five years and trained 365 days a year, sometimes swimming multiple times a day. His one hundred percent commitment put him far beyond every other swimmer, and he won twenty-three gold medals, making him the all-time gold medal winner swimmer. I don't believe Michael Phelps woke up each day and had to decide if he was going to swim practice or not. That decision and firm commitment was already a way of life for him.

If you determine in advance that you'll be one hundred percent committed, then you've decided once and for all,

and you don't need to revisit that decision again. It's much harder to be ninety-eight percent committed because you'll continually need to remake the decision every time a new scenario arises.

People offer me alcohol several times a week it seems, at a business lunch, at conferences, parties, and other events, but I have no temptation to drink because I've already committed to my choice. People offer to buy me a drink or ask me what I'm drinking, and they really want to treat me. I can simply tell them I don't drink and I'll stick to my water. It's not ever context-dependent; it's an across-the-board commitment. I'm no longer even mildly curious, because I've set my standard firmly and am sticking to it.

> *"At one point in time, I would say that drinking too much when I would hang out with friends was probably my biggest temptation. The biggest impact it has had on my life is a LOT of wasted money and me not showing up one hundred percent because I was hungover.*
>
> *Currently, I no longer have what I consider negative temptations from a health standpoint. By being honest with myself, I have been able to enjoy things in moderation and maintain a high level of health and fitness. I also am a lifelong martial artist, and I have always found a lot of confidence in my physical fitness and physical skills. I think my belief that physical and mental health are the*

foundation of everything has always kept me very healthy."

— MARK CHOE // OWNER & GENERAL
MANAGER OF THE PINES RESORT

THE MYTH OF WILLPOWER

People with big goals often mistakenly believe they can be in an environment that runs counter to their vision but somehow resist temptation. **You feel strong, motivated, and disciplined, so it seems unnecessary to avoid things altogether. But I'll let you in on a secret: eventually, willpower dies.**

You might resist temptation for a time, but if you keep exposing yourself to what you're trying to resist, you'll eventually give in. If you're trying to avoid gambling, you can't sit in a casino for days at a time and expect not to give in. Maybe you think you can just play the slots with a handful of quarters and call it good, but you also may wake up in your fifties completely financially destitute because you've gambled away all your retirement savings. I know of people who squandered millions of dollars because of their gambling addiction. The casinos aren't stupid; they keep the lights on for a reason. If you have that predilection, they'll wear you down if given the chance.

What tempts me will be different from what tempts you based on our weaknesses and social inclinations, but the

core message is the same: **avoiding temptation is easier than resisting it.** Particular activities are riskier for some people than others. Some people might be hardcore spenders who jeopardize their future financial freedom, while others are hardcore drinkers who damage their health. Some people feel compelled to eat ice cream every night at midnight while vegging out in front of the TV, which will catch up to their health, too.

 "A man's true character is revealed by what he does when no one is watching."

— UNKNOWN

So how do we avoid the temptations? Recognize and identify the temptations that will prevent you from creating incredible personal health and significant legacy wealth. Then, avoid those temptations entirely. Be honest with yourself. **Don't put yourself in environments where it's easy to justify or give in to your weaknesses. Instead, turn your weaknesses into strengths by learning more about yourself, your fears, the triggers for your bad decisions, and the situations that help you move closer to your goals instead of undermining them.**

Dr. Benjamin Hardy wrote a book on this subject of setting up your environment for success: it's called *Willpower Doesn't Work*. The book argues for setting up our physical and mental environment for success by being intentional about what we expose our bodies and minds to. If we put ourselves in a context that encourages our success, instead of forcing us to constantly hold the line against temptation, we can work with the positive momentum rather than draining our energy.

Avoiding means you don't even see, let alone visit, the donut shop, while resisting means walking by the donut shop every day and using willpower not to go inside, or even worse, keeping a box of donuts in your kitchen but telling yourself you won't eat any. If you rely on resisting, eventually you'll give in. Discipline and habits work long-term, but relying alone on willpower is not sustainable. It will always wear down. Changing your environment to support your goals and habits is far better than trying to rely on willpower.

At the time of this writing, the sobriety movement is on the rise, even among people who do not meet the criteria for an alcohol abuse disorder. In general, people have an increasing interest in self-regulation, which is another way of saying keeping personal commitments to yourself. If you can regulate yourself in situations, then you can make better decisions for yourself and thereby have better outcomes.

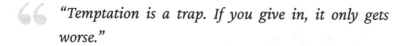 *"Temptation is a trap. If you give in, it only gets worse."*

— UNKNOWN

Our identity and mindset are determined by the stories we tell ourselves. Tony Robbins says we make decisions based on our identity—who we believe we are. If you say to yourself, "I'm an athlete," you will eat and work out differently than if you say, "I'm a video gamer." **Whatever you believe will reinforce the internal story that guides your behavior, making that belief come true.**

You have already reached a certain level of success based on your beliefs. The next level is having full clarity that the words "I am..." represent the most powerful identity-reinforcing behavior there is. What is your belief about yourself and your identity? Do you keep your commitments to yourself? What are your boundaries?

Right now, I'm on a health quest. It's a quest because I'm actively pursuing the path, excited about it, and aiming for a major goal. If I had a donut or a huge piece of cake today, I would not feel as good about myself tomorrow. I'd feel like I'd let myself down. When you keep your commitments, your confidence rises. If you slip up, there's an issue with the story you're telling yourself. The good news is that you hold the power to change that story and course-correct right away.

Even highly successful people can suffer from imposter syndrome. You might outwardly state that you want to lose weight but inwardly decide you're not capable. Because that self-defeating story is running through your head, when you hit a setback, it's easy to see the setback as the truth about your capability or worthiness.

Don't fall into that trap.

"Earlier in my career, I looked at headlines a lot. My emotions and confidence were affected. I no longer fall into this temptation.

These days I can be overly optimistic about new technological breakthroughs, although I don't make big financial decisions based upon these breakthroughs... I do my thinking ahead of time so I don't need to deal with decision fatigue in the moment and suffer from regret."

— KARY OBERBRUNNER // BESTSELLING
AUTHOR OF TWELVE BOOKS, CEO OF
IGNITING SOULS & BLOCKCHAIN LIFE

SURROUND YOURSELF WITH SUPPORT

Because our inner monologue needs reinforcement to stay positive, no matter how much you've already achieved, it's important to put yourself in a position to be held accountable and encouraged. **No one is perfect, bulletproof, or disciplined one hundred percent of the time; we're all susceptible to temptation. Surround yourself with people who genuinely want what's best for you and will help you avoid your temptations while enforcing your boundaries and commitments. Those types of relationships are golden.**

We also need to be intentional about who we spend time with and the media we consume. Everything we let into our lives impacts and influences us. Based on the information and attitudes around you, will you make short-term or long-term decisions? A short-term mindset says, "This donut is going to taste really good. It's just one donut. Eat the donut." Or, "It's just one workout today or just one exercise I'm skipping. If I miss, it's not a big deal." In that mindset, one negative choice can quickly spiral into six months of donuts and no workouts. At the end of the year, you're a completely different person, and not for the better—all because of a momentary thought that your actions don't really matter.

It would be so easy for me to be ninety-eight percent committed and decide celebrating a big business deal is worth a sip of alcohol. It won't hurt anyone. Maybe not, but six months later, I could also find I'm addicted, consuming more calories than I want, feeling too sluggish to take action on my goals, or negatively impacted in a host of different ways.

So don't let a short moment, no matter the circumstances, overtake your decisions and commitments to yourself—and the people in your inner circle who support you.

"Avoiding temptations and seeking the help of others (and a higher power) have transformed my life, and so has remaining disciplined each day about what my objective is. And in this particular context, that objective is for me to not drink or to put other substances in my body. That level of discipline has provided me with freedom and has made it where it's no longer a concern in my life at all. It's gotten quite easy with practice: to wake up and simply not to drink. It also provides me with great joy to be able to share that experience with others and help them along their paths.

When I look back at it, many of the things that I value the most in my life come with a great deal of practice. And that practice requires discipline and support, whether it's with my personal nutrition each day or with my relationship with my wife, which also requires a great deal of practice, commitment, and discipline.

These things also provide me with great joy—and I could not do any of them if I hadn't gotten to where I am today."

— KEEGAN CALDWELL

DON'T LET SHORT-TERM EMOTIONS STEER YOUR SHIP

As with indulging and skipping exercise, there are a million short-term temptations with wealth. For instance, people constantly want to sell investments when the stock market is down and the economy is in turmoil. They get scared, but that short-sighted decision has permanent, negative impacts. Many people make decisions based on their feelings in the moment, rather than their goals for the long term. **When you make money decisions based on your fleeting feelings, you'll always be wrong. In investing, natural instinct typically runs counter to what you should actually do.**

Everyone cites the mantra "buy low, sell high," meaning buy investments when they're cheap and sell them when they're expensive. However, almost everyone does the exact opposite. They succumb to emotion instead of acting based on long-term principles and strategies.

You would never consciously decide to go to Nordstrom and buy the new suits as soon as they triple in price. That's not the time to fill up your closet with new suits. However, people engage in that exact behavior with their investments. They wait until a stock triples in price and then load up, instead of waiting for it to drop fifty or seventy-five percent and loading up at a discount. Waiting until something is popular before buying or selling when there's a dip in popularity leads to irrational, money-losing decisions.

Don't fall victim to that temptation with your money.

Heidi Cortez, a marketing entrepreneur in Los Angeles, CA, has lived through and learned from a scenario like this. She invested in "hot" stocks and cryptocurrencies, following the trends of what everyone else was talking about. "On one 'hot' stock, I made a lot of money, so I invested more... and that backfired," she said. "I ended up losing seventy percent very quickly."

A PANDEMIC LESSON

In March 2020, the stock market dropped forty percent in less than a month. That was a scary time for people in terms of both health and wealth, as an unfamiliar virus raged and the value of financial savings that they had worked so hard to accumulate declined. I know someone who was terrified of losing more and thought their investments would drop to zero if they didn't take action.

So they completely liquidated their portfolio after it had declined forty percent. They knew all the investing advice they'd ever known said that was a terrible idea, and we'd even discussed it together personally. But they proceeded with selling everything anyway, saying they'd wait to invest until they felt more comfortable and the market outlook was better. The decision ran completely counter to their written investment strategy guide and my professional advice.

As it turned out, not only did the stock market recover that forty percent loss, it also rose far above its previous high before the pandemic was close to being over. My friend stayed uninvested through the stock market rebounds of 2020 and 2021 with their money on the sidelines, watching the market go up and up and up, thinking maybe it would come back down.

The problem? When COVID-19 hit in 2020 and the whole world shut down, the S&P 500 still grew by 16.3 percent for that year, which is an incredible year. No one would have predicted that kind of growth under those circumstances. Then, in 2021, the market had a twenty-seven percent positive return. So anyone who decided to get back into the market after selling low had to buy high, the exact opposite of a money-making strategy. Both 2020 and 2021 were pandemic years, but they returned more than a forty percent growth in value.

People couldn't have predicted that exact trajectory, but they could have stayed the course with their longer-term strategy and benefited by simply staying invested instead of letting their fear steer their decision-making. **The problem is when you start making emotional, short-term decisions, it's hard to get back on track. It's like having a rudderless ship and no map.** The winds—in this case, emotions—push you wherever they may, without you charting your own course. When you lose the rudder of your rational planning and decision-making, you put yourself at the mercy of external forces.

EMBRACE SOME UNCERTAINTY

When it comes to health care and wealth care, you won't see instant results even from the best choices. If you eat healthy and exercise today, you won't notice a difference. If you keep at it, though, in a couple years, you'll notice significant change, maybe a complete transformation. It's the same with creating wealth. You have to make choices with faith in the future, knowing you probably won't see results for a long time. That delayed reward is exactly why most people don't follow through with their goals. Because they don't see instant results, they decide to take the easy route and satisfy instant gratification, asking only what feels or tastes good right in the moment to get a dopamine hit.

If you're an entrepreneur, you likely already have a propensity for risk and making decisions that involve uncertainty. Use that to your advantage! Too many people want certainty. They want to know exactly how an investment will turn out. They want to have their entire career path spelled out for them. They want to know exactly what salary they can expect in five years if they get a certain degree and complete particular tasks. Predictability offers a sense of stability. But that's not always how life works.

An entrepreneur like you is willing to accept unpredictability and uncertainty, making decisions without knowing exactly how they'll turn out. If you trust the process with uncertainty, you'll have higher upside and higher rewards. You're part of that one percent. You take on those greater rewards because most of the world is unwilling to wrestle with that discomfort and uncertainty. Make sure you're leveraging that ability to its full extent for both your health and your wealth.

Of course, there's a difference between being uncomfortable with uncertainty and taking unnecessary risks. **Avoiding temptation includes staying away from get-rich-quick schemes and avoiding jumping on the bandwagon of trendy financial investments.** You probably have a dozen friends and colleagues recommending investment opportunities all the time, which are a particular form of temptation. You're successful, but you're still just as susceptible to temptation and making bad financial decisions in the moment as anyone else.

My job security is high because I'm good at preventing people from making those bad choices and big mistakes. My role at Pacific Capital is to keep our high-net-worth entrepreneur clients committed to their long-term strategies and goals, despite the extreme uncertainty and emotions in the moment. It's like mindset coaching for your money and your business. My extreme discipline and commitment style are good for entrepreneurs who are used to taking the lead and making split-second decisions.

Sometimes, you need an expert to tell you no, that your impulse isn't productive and there's a better way, one that avoids unnecessary mistakes. No matter how much you've earned and achieved, you can still use accountability and coaching to prevent irrational, short-term decisions that will hurt you in the long run—especially if most people in your life are afraid to speak bluntly. My clients appreciate my candor, because they don't get it in many areas of their lives.

> " *The only way to avoid temptation is to have a strong sense of purpose and self-discipline.* "
>
> — UNKNOWN

TURN YOUR WEAKNESSES INTO STRENGTHS

Recall my friend Keegan, the Iraq veteran who faced addiction and PTSD? Those *were* his weaknesses, but now they're his strengths. He is so self-aware of his propensity to be addicted to substances that he still attends these meetings weekly, ten years later. In fact, once, we were on vacation with a group of friends, and he left dinner early to keep his weekly commitment to attend the AA meeting on zoom. I was blown away. But he knows that consistency keeps him on track and sober, and it's also what allows him to mentor people and stay strong.

Keegan is strong and successful, while also seeing where he could become weak in the future—and taking active steps to stay on track. That's what it takes.

On the wealth side, it's important to take a beat when you encounter new, exciting-sounding opportunities. Have the self-awareness to pause and get an expert opinion instead of just reacting.

For example, I have a client who gets so excited about new investment opportunities that he wants to put $100,000 down on the spot. He's a very optimistic, fun, enthusiastic entrepreneur. I put some boundaries in place and told him he needed to stop saying yes in the moment, because many of the investments didn't work out. We came up with a plan in which he agreed to include Pacific Capital and his wife in any potential investment conversation before making a decision or commitment. Instead of saying yes or no, he now tells people who pitch him that the opportunity sounds interesting, but he first needs to speak to his financial team and his spouse. Having this strategy in place is more powerful than having him rely on "willpower" alone.

Know what tempts you, and set up the guardrails and accountability to avoid temptation while turning your weaknesses into strengths.

Embrace the fact that consistency is greater than motivation and willpower. You can't only do the right thing when you feel like it, because more often than not, you won't feel like it.

In addition, try these tips:

• Be honest with yourself about temptation. Cheating when others aren't looking only harms yourself.

 – Write a list of three temptations that you constantly fall back into and create boundaries about how to avoid them going forward. Share your new boundaries and ask for support from the five people closest to you.

 – Ask yourself questions like "What, if anything, are you avoiding admitting to yourself?" and "When it comes to making financial decisions, do you listen more to a team of experts or amateurs/your ego?"

 – Don't inhale your own success. Ask for help when you need it.

• Practice self-care and mindfulness. You must take care of yourself physically, mentally, and emotionally to avoid temptation. When you're tired and fatigued, you are weaker and more susceptible to giving into temptation and getting off track.

— Track your sleep and ensure that at least five nights a week, you're sleeping at least eight hours. Set an alarm that reminds you what time to start your bedtime routine. Plug in your phone far away from your bed. Drink water first thing when you wake up to hydrate to avoid starting your day with a poor meal choice.

— Schedule time on your calendar for meditation, prayer, sauna, massages... anything that helps put you in a relaxed state of mind every week.

— Practice box breathing (a self-care technique). This stills your mind and heart and puts you in a better state to make decisions and avoid temptation.

— Clear out all previously purchased tempting items. Throw away the alcohol, cigarettes, donuts, etc. Don't keep it in the cupboard or fridge if it's a temptation.

"If you think it's expensive to hire a professional to do the job, wait until you hire an amateur."

– RED ADAIR

3
HIRE ONLY TOP EXPERTS

I may be an expert in wealth building, but I'm not above being coached and trained. I'm so thankful for the help of an expert in health building. I'm not just giving this advice in this book because it sounds good; I really do practice what I preach.

At the time of this writing, I'm still down forty-five pounds from my high-water mark on the rooftop in Denver. Having accountability partners and expert coaches to correct me when I get off course is critical to the progress I've made. Twice a week, we FaceTime each other and we review my report, which includes everything I've eaten, my workouts, my weight and my sleep. There are weeks where I'm excited and others where I'm embarrassed and wishing I could hide. But that's part of the deal: hire the experts who will keep you accountable and teach you how to get back on track when you slip up. Also, my trainer lives in London and we've never met in person. So you've got no excuse; you can use technology and find an expert that fits your needs from literally anywhere in the world.

Expert coaching keeps you on track because it provides structure rather than relying on individual motivation alone. If you tell someone you want to change, you're more likely to follow through. My coach also gives me suggestions based on my goals and upcoming schedule. For instance, I was going to go on a couples' trip to Bora Bora with college friends and their spouses, so he planned out my workouts and diet in the weeks leading up to that gathering. Because he's an expert, if he knows the target, he can tailor the path to get me there. He didn't make me skip all the fun meals there, but he gave me enough guidance and encouragement to stay within some boundaries so I wouldn't be too far off track when we came back home.

Once you've made your commitments, a coach helps keep you accountable because those commitments are public. If you hire a personal trainer, you're paying them to teach you, coach you, encourage you, and keep you accountable. It would be a real shame for you to pay for coaching and not follow through on what they're telling you to do. In my case, for the weeks I slacked off, getting on that FaceTime call and owning up to it was pretty motivating to do better the following week.

Proper coaching offers support, encouragement, discipline, accountability, feedback, and structure to ensure you do what you say you'll do. That expertise with personal guidance helps you set and maintain the small daily habits that lead to the big gains. Success requires some structure and predictability. These are born of your routines and habits, which are supported by coaching and accountability.

THE VALUE OF FEEDBACK

Achieving next-level health and wealth both require being open to feedback and using it to improve. **The most successful people are teachable and humble. On the other hand, know-it-alls have mediocre coaches or more often, no coaches at all. They think they can do it all themselves because of their pride and ego.**

One of the greatest skills you can possess is the ability to ask for help when you need it. If you're the smartest or the most successful person in the room every day, you're in the wrong room. If you want to be successful, surround yourself with people who are more successful than you. Hire the best people you can find, and give them the freedom to do their work.

In both sports and business, the best of the best are the most coachable. No matter how successful they get, they still have coaches and mentors. Michael Mogul is a client of mine; he owns an incredibly successful law firm coaching business called Crisp, based in Atlanta, Georgia. He personally spent $8 million to put on the biggest industry conference for lawyers in the country last year. Despite leading the coaching industry, he is also extremely coachable. He takes our team's financial advice, and he takes my advice on health and fitness. He hired my same trainer and has seen phenomenal results in just a few short months. The keys to his success and growth are that he seeks out expert feedback, implements it, and always strives to improve. He doesn't hesitate and doesn't let his ego prevent him from taking advice.

On his podcast, Michael recently interviewed Tim Grover, who personally coached Michael Jordan and then Kobe Bryant—arguably two of the top five basketball players ever —through their entire careers. Tim is completely credited with helping them reach the level of success they did. He talked about the principles of a winning mindset, using emotional intelligence, and how to succeed in the face of big challenges. These two elite players had the same coach, which is not a coincidence. Everyone worships the ground they've walked on, but they were coachable. No matter how good they got, they listened to the experts and understood the value of having someone knowledgeable identify their weak spots and how they could change and improve.

They had someone to confide in when they struggled. They had someone to ask advice from before high-pressure moments. They never thought that they had all the answers.

Not only did they have access to someone willing to give them that feedback, but their personalities were such that they were *willing to take it.* **Experts can give you advice all day long, but it does no good unless you listen.**

"Great vision without great people is irrelevant."

— JIM COLLINS

WHY YOU NEED AN EXPERT

You're a leader in so many areas, **but it's time to fire your-self as the CEO of your health and wealth.**

We have a very successful client who accumulated close to $20 million of investable dollars by the time he was in his mid-thirties, primarily by buying their own mutual funds and having some robo-advisor accounts, which essentially automate investment choices when you make deposits in your account. Those strategies make sense for people who are not making much money because they simplify and auto-mate the investment process. Eventually, though, the client realized they had outgrown themselves as their own DIY financial team. We did a Full Financial Life Inspection® and found many opportunities to increase investment cash flow, decrease income taxes, and increase growth opportunities in the investment portfolio—all while relieving this client of the time and hassle of managing their financial life on his own.

Their greatest non-financial goals as a couple for the year were to increase free time, improve health, and take away the stress that they had experienced the previous year. Not only did we improve their financial life and all the different cate-gories of family protection with insurance planning and estate planning, but we also helped educate their business employees, hire a new CFO, reduce their taxes and improve their cash flow *while removing the stress and the burden of doing the work themselves.* They have so much more free time and reduced stress, which contributes to your health and how you feel about life.

I have hundreds of stories of clients who thought they were achieving great results on the DIY track (or they thought they already had all the expertise they needed in a basic financial advisor). Once they had a deeper conversation with our team, though, it became clear they'd outgrown the level of expertise that had once served them. As their net worth grew and their financial lives became more complex, they didn't realize their needs had outstripped the skills and expertise of the professionals they'd hired a long time ago.

If you hired a tax accountant and a financial advisor in the early stages of your career when you were barely starting out, but now you're a founder-entrepreneur whose business has grown 20x since you started your wealth planning, you definitely should look around and see what's out there to meet you at your higher level of complexity.

You shouldn't be DIY-ing your health or your wealth. If you want to reach high levels of success, implement the "who not how" principle from Dan Sullivan: Don't ask, "*How* can I reach extremely high levels of success and achievement?" Instead, ask, "*Who* can help me get there?"

"*My most significant commitment to myself is to be a person of my word in all aspects of life. To keep myself accountable, I have found the right people to help me. These accountability partners have been my insurance policy to ensure that I am following through on my promises. They have been my cheerleaders, supporting me when things are going well, but more importantly, they have been willing to call me out when things are not going according to plan. Their support has allowed me to reflect on my actions, improve, and keep moving forward towards my goals.*

I haven't always turned to experts as accountability partners, though. For years, I attempted to handle my company's finances on my own in an effort to cut costs. However, it wasn't until two years ago when I outsourced these responsibilities that I realized the true cost in terms of time and money.

Hiring an experienced accountant and financial advisor has allowed me to maximize my tax efficiency, invest my funds to generate compound interest, and ultimately achieve greater financial freedom.

Not only that, but by freeing up my time, I have been able to concentrate on my true passion as an online fitness coach, providing better service to more clients and enhancing retention rates."

— RYAN STEVENS MSC // ONLINE FITNESS
COACH

Collaboration is the key to success. You can't be an expert in everything, but you can build a team of experts who can help you achieve your goals. You just have to have access to people who are great at what you're not.

That expertise won't be cheap, but it doesn't matter if you get the results you're aiming for. The help isn't unaffordable; you get what you pay for. In fact, I can't afford *not* to get that expertise because of the impact it'll have on your future. It's an investment, not a cost.

The bottom line is that by engaging an expert, you can accelerate growth, save time, and, in the long run, save money. In the end, you'll achieve your goals more quickly and effectively than you otherwise would.

OUTGROWING PROFESSIONALS

It's okay to outgrow a relationship with an expert and decide to level up. You likely know that on some level, but that's not the same as internalizing it. Let's take a closer look.

We often meet clients who hired a tax professional straight out of college, and they're still using that person even though their business is now doing $50 million or $250 million a year in annual revenues. I can almost guarantee that this accountant who was working with a recent college graduate likely doesn't have the experience or the expertise to give strategic tax planning advice to a business owner running a $250-million-a-year company.

This dynamic is more than hypothetical. I worked with a client who was going through the complex sale of his company and was working with his local tax person in the community to do his bookkeeping and file his annual returns. Had he done no strategic planning before the business sale, it would have cost him an extra $5 million to $10 million in taxes. Fortunately, we introduced him to a team that could help. Choosing to engage with this team that specialized in business transactions specific to his business size and industry meant he could structure the deal with the buyer in a way that allowed him and his family to keep that extra money. This goes to show that hiring experts who are *at your level* is crucial. Just like there's very different training for an Ironman World Championships versus your local 5K charity run, there's a very big difference between a tax preparer who simply prepares tax returns and a professional team who does strategic planning.

At Pacific Capital, we help clients recognize and understand who they've outgrown in their circle of advisors. **A sure sign you've outgrown your financial team is if you're**

suggesting different tax strategies and planning to your professional, rather than the other way around. The experts should be initiating the ideas and strategies, not relying on the client to do so.

> *"Outgrowing an expert that has been tremendously valuable can be a challenging situation. In my experience, this has usually been the result of the client's needs growing beyond the scope of what the expert could offer or desired to grow into offering. In such circumstances, finding a new expert with the knowledge to meet your expanded needs as a client is usually the easy part. Sharing that reality with gratitude and appreciation for what you have accomplished with the original expert is usually the hard part.*

> *I've witnessed many of these conversations, and they seem to go best by simply being honest with the original expert. If the relationship was built the right way from the outset, while it will be hard for the original expert to hear, it will offer them valuable perspective on the limits of their current practice (something they will thank you for later, as it gives them impetus to choose to pursue growth in the future or affirm their limits).*

And because it was done with honesty and care, it will accomplish such without severing communication and a professional (and potentially even personal) relationship that may exist and be desired going forward."

— MATT MUNSON // FOUNDER OF SERVANT
FINANCIAL LLC

As that case study above, we also work with DIYers who've accumulated great wealth and outgrown themselves. They need to fire themselves as the financial investment team because their financial assets and income have grown too big to handle on their own. Think of it this way: you might be able to do a great job painting your own first apartment, but if you're moving into a 10,000-square-foot-mansion estate, painting the walls of that entire property is beyond your capacity and skill level. You need to hire a team that paints big houses for a living. You've leveled up since your younger years and find yourself in a new situation with different needs today. Be sure you have the best of the best around you, because the consequences of how you manage your money and your health are serious and long-lasting.

Here are some other reasons to upgrade:

- Having experts on your team keeps you competitive and engaged.
- Top experts stay up-to-date on the latest developments and strategies, which keeps you ahead of the curve and helps avoid stagnation.
- If you're with the same person, they may not be advancing at an adequate pace to keep up with you. I find holdovers from earlier stages of life often aren't advancing. They're stagnant and complacent, which holds clients back. You need someone who will develop new techniques and methods to keep you going forward.
- You expand your network, build relationships, and get new insights.
- The environment is constantly changing, and you need to have top experts who are also evolving, developing, and growing.

My team is constantly growing and exploring the cutting edge of our field. I love to hire and add talented people to our team, so we can dig into newer, bigger, better strategies, which impacts the advice we give clients. If you hire a firm where the advisor is just coasting in cruise control and wants to keep the same clients they've always had while focusing on their golf game, you won't get fresh ideas about building wealth.

RECOGNIZING EXPERTISE

Now that we've established the value of the right experts, how do you find them? First, check client references and reviews, and then look for personal evidence of the experts implementing their advice in their own life.

Why is this important? Simple: experts need to practice what they preach. Too often, people take advice from others who haven't achieved what they're trying to achieve or reached the level where they are. **It's important to hire a trainer who eats healthy food and is in excellent shape; it's important to hire a financial advisor who has achieved what you want to achieve with your business and finances.** Any financial advisor had better not be struggling financially, doling out advice while in debt themselves. During my time at Merrill Lynch, there was an older financial advisor who put on a very showy facade of wealth with his fancy watches, suits, and cars, and yet he was actually living in an apartment complex and buried in personal credit card debt. His net worth was below $0 with his credit card debt and non-existent savings, yet he was giving financial advice under the guise of being very successful personally. If a "financial professional" is disorganized, stressed or shows no wealth-building success on their own, they likely won't have what it takes to get you to your next level up.

"Hiring and working with the best experts is critical. For me, this is a must as I want to be the best version of myself and believe that I can only become that if I can learn from the best. This comes from a belief that I have had from a very young age: if you want to have the best mentor, you have to be the best mentee because the best mentors are looking for the best mentees.

There are lots of examples throughout my life where I have put this into practice:

<u>Business:</u> I have two business coaches with whom I spend significant time and have added a Board of Directors including three super-competent people who provide guidance when it comes to scaling Genioo. This team can see the forest from the trees, which is hard to do when you're in the thick of it, and give me access to years of collective experience with just a few hours of their time.

<u>Spirituality:</u> I have two coaches who are very deep in spirituality. These mentors are so advanced that every time I engage with them, it makes me realize how much room I have to grow and improve.

Personal Life: I have also decided to use experts in areas of my life in which I do not need to be an expert. This is a model that is closer to 'managed services,' which allows me to benefit from the most important information in some of the most important areas of my life without having to become an expert myself. This is the case for my wealth which is managed by Pacific Capital and for my Fitness which is managed by Supra Human and my Health by Fountain Life."

— FREDERIC BRUNNER // FOUNDER, CEO, AND CHAIRMAN OF THE GENIOO GROUP; CO-FOUNDER OF LOMBARD REAL ESTATE

While you're on your search, remember that it's not the years of experience that matter but rather *the quality* of their experience. Look for experts who can demonstrate results, both in their clients and themselves personally.

My personal trainer is a physical specimen who's lifting much heavier than I am and that motivates me to work harder. He'll occasionally send me a text from his gym or a picture of himself headed to a workout, even when it's negative ten degrees and snowing at 4:30 in the morning. If he can persevere under those circumstances, then who am I to skip my workout in my comfortable home gym?

For wealth building, if you're a growth-focused entrepreneur, you want to take financial advice from experts who have personally built wealth as entrepreneurs and are at or above the level that you're trying to achieve yourself. You'll grow and progress much quicker by paying the premium required for the right experts on your team than you will by trying to cut corners and save costs with mediocre coaches or the DIY approach.

If you want to be ridiculously ambitious and achieve your goals, you need to be willing to pay for the worthwhile value for the right experts to be on your team, both in health coaching and in wealth coaching. These are not areas to go cheap. Your personal health and your financial legacy and wealth building are worth more than finding someone random online.

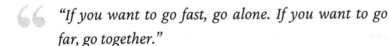 *"If you want to go fast, go alone. If you want to go far, go together."*

— AFRICAN PROVERB

METRICS MATTER

Management theorist Peter Drucker said what gets measured gets improved. When it comes to your health situation and your financial portfolio, you have to be willing to look at the numbers *as they are and where they're actually going* rather than simply thinking about them in an aspirational way.

If you're more of a lone wolf or a DIY person, it's important to foster coachability in yourself. We've addressed the value of this, but how do you do it? First, I recommend allowing yourself and your current circumstances to be assessed. For financial clients at Pacific Capital, we do a Financial Life Inspection®, where we dig deep into all of their family and business financials. It's like going to the doctor. You think you're in good shape and that you're healthy, but until you go to the doctor and theoretically (and/or literally) take your pants down, you don't really know. You need to get your blood drawn and take all the external and internal physical tests.

The same goes for your financial health. Have someone look at five years of tax returns. **You have no clue about your own blind spots; that's why they're blind spots. If you think you know it all and your financial life is in perfect order, at least get confirmation by having a third-party expert do an assessment. What do you have to lose?**

If nothing's wrong, they'll confirm how amazing you are and that your money is being optimized in every area of your business, your investments, and inside your family's financial plan. And if there are problems, they'll help you fix them. Either way, you win. Until you get that clarity through cold hard metrics, you're living in fantasy land. If you think you've accessed everything there is to know by reading articles online or watching things on YouTube, you're only fooling yourself. None of the greats have gotten there without having experts and coaches on their team. None of them.

You can't be an expert in everything, so it's important to seek out expertise in the areas that aren't your personal niche. When you seek out that level of support from experts, you'll exponentially increase your results. The biggest, hardest step is asking for help in the first place.

FACE THE TRUTH

Be willing to face the truth of what you don't want to hear because often, it's what you need to hear. You might have a hard time with criticism, even when it's constructive. But it's important to accept that temporary discomfort if you want to grow, to improve and become more coachable. **No matter how smart you are, you shouldn't always feel like the smartest person in every room. And if that's the case, you need to change rooms.**

You can't take constructive criticism personally if you're trying to get better. It's not an attack on your abilities or your character. In fact, it's intended to help you improve and grow, so you actually need to seek out more of it. The best and highest achievers continually seek input to improve. If you're willing to actively listen and even show appreciation for that feedback, you'll receive more of it, which will accelerate your growth. In sports, your coach or your trainer is giving you feedback and pointing out your mistakes because they want you to improve. I can't imagine a good coach that makes no corrections during an entire practice on the basketball court.

People often share financial mistakes or bad habits that they're very embarrassed about. They're almost ashamed to admit them out loud. Having areas that need major improvement doesn't undermine your worth as a person. Rather, it's just feedback from decisions you've made in the past and how you can make better ones in the future. That information is a valuable gift. You can use it to create positive future outcomes, seeing criticism as an opportunity to learn and grow. Approach constructive feedback with an open mind and a willingness to receive it and improve. If you feel defensive, recognize that as a signal that you're in a scarcity mindset, which stunts your growth.

This concept connects to *The Four Agreements: A Practical Guide to Personal Freedom* by Don Miguel Ruiz. In that framework, the second agreement is not to take anything personally. That stance mitigates suffering while allowing you to live life on a higher level, one where you're free.

 "The wise learn from the experience of others, while fools learn only from their own."

— AFRICAN PROVERB

In choosing an expert, keep the following in mind:

• Do your due diligence. Ask for recommendations, and confirm that the expert has achieved what you want to achieve—and isn't just doling out advice they don't follow themselves.

 — Identify the areas where you're stuck. Seek out the top experts in that field. If you don't know who they are, ask for referrals or recommendations from others who have already achieved it themselves.

• Recognize the value of using data and metrics to measure progress and growth.

 — Decide what 2–3 metrics would be most important for you to measure, starting today, from where you are to where you want to go. (For example, I measure hours slept each night, weight, protein consumed daily, body fat percentage, monthly passive income, annual business profits, and dollars saved and invested monthly.)

• Cultivate coachability. You cannot DIY next-level success.

 — Ask your two most trusted friends to name your

blind spots and weaknesses. Write down the things you can identify that you need to work on... what areas would you love to have an expert guiding you? Avoid defensiveness and use the feedback as fuel.

"Innovation distinguishes between a leader and a follower. Embracing new technology is a key component of innovation."

– STEVE JOBS

4

TRANSFORM WITH TECHNOLOGY

Twenty-two years ago, there was a very well-known cosmetic surgeon from Newport Beach, California, who earned an income of over $1 million per year and had all the right status symbols of success—a fancy beach house, a red Lamborghini, a beautiful vacation home in Hawaii, all the nicest business suits and brand name ties, you name it. He was fifty-five years old at the time and feeling pretty good about himself and the first-class life he'd created.

He came into his first appointment with me saying he wanted to retire by age sixty-two. "But I'm doing so well, and my practice is growing so quickly," he reported, "that I think I'd like to retire by age sixty. Play some more golf, travel the world, do whatever I feel like doing!" He was pretty excited about this, knowing it was potentially only five years away.

Given that accelerated timeline, he wanted to see what he should do with his investments and how we could help. Over the following two weeks, our team conducted a deep dive into his situation, similar to a Financial Life Inspection®. We discovered that based on his goals, wants, and needs, he could not retire at age sixty as he'd hoped. In fact, he couldn't even retire by age sixty-five because of his high lifestyle spending expectations.

He was spending way too much today, not saving much at all, and had overextended himself with debt in order to keep "living the good life" of a rich surgeon in Newport Beach. He had massive loans that were piling up. Even his less ambitious retirement age of sixty-two wasn't achievable. Without doing this deep financial health check-up with us, he would've continued on his merry way thinking everything was cool and that he'd be prepared for a lavish life of golf and entertainment in just a few short years with his other retired friends. Until he went through the inspection and we put the numbers on paper, he somehow believed he was ahead of schedule, when he wasn't even on schedule at all. In his mind, because his income was growing each year, he was doing well and had nothing to worry about. Yet he was extremely behind where he could've been, based on how much his income grew in the previous decade. The harsh reality was that he'd need to make some drastic changes to even retire by sixty-five.

Talking with us gave him a major wake-up call. He was understandably disappointed, and it was a difficult conversation. However, we were able to help him make some significant adjustments to prepare for a successful retirement and get back on track.

The technology and tools that we used to forecast his financial life into the future and assess the costs of his debt were extremely useful to give him the visual picture of the cash flow problem at hand. That assessment helped him finally face the truth, without which he would've encountered a terrible, negative surprise when he reached his ideal retirement age. It would've been a disaster.

 "The most important thing that you can do is not to waste the opportunity that technology is giving you."

— PRIYANKA CHOPRA // ACTOR &
ENTREPRENEUR

MANAGING THE "WHAT IFS"

On the flip side, a client came to us and, despite having significant wealth, felt they didn't have enough and was constantly worried that their family would struggle and suffer if something happened to him. He felt pressure to keep working in a stressful and unpleasant job environment, while being extremely frugal with his spending for fear of running out of money. They had grown up without enough money and carried that feeling of scarcity into their adult life, even though resources were no longer scarce. The voice of their parents asking—*How do you think we can afford that? You think money grows on trees? Do you know how much I pay for this?*—was always in the back of their minds.

Though they were extremely wealthy, with millions of dollars, low monthly expenses, and no debt, they refused to believe that they had achieved financial freedom and security. In particular, the husband was always laser-focused on how much every little thing cost, and he spread his money anxiety to the whole family. They simply could not accept or believe that they'd be okay and lived as if everything was about to fall apart. It seemed to them like around every corner there was an impending disaster that would take all their money away and they'd be broke again.

Once we went through their assessment, we were able to show them that even if he quit his job and her entire business collapsed and every worst-case scenario happened simultaneously, they'd still be totally fine. They could still live more comfortably than they were currently living without a care in the world. For the first time ever, seeing it like this, they actually believed it. There was a palpable change in the husband's countenance in particular—a relaxing of the shoulders and relief of the stress and anxiety. The couple could finally believe that they'd be okay, and they could let go of that heavy burden of stress they'd been carrying all this time.

They saw how robust their financial foundation was and the advanced tools that showed how financially secure they actually were. We showed them all the different sources of cash flow, some even insured, and the surplus of assets in many diversified investments. Going through a technology-assisted professional assessment totally changed their marriage, the general mood in their family, and their attitude toward life. They became more hopeful and positive, less worried all the time. Before, they'd feel stress over the simplest expenses, like going to a restaurant for dinner, which was completely unnecessary in the context of their wealth.

No one could persuade them emotionally to feel differently, but we could provide objective, third-party data based on our technology and expertise that finally made them feel okay. They've completely transformed, and that Financial Life Inspection® changed their life.

Knowing exactly where you stand allows you to make tangible progress toward your goals and live a lifestyle of freedom and ease, which contributes to your physical and mental health and wellness. As I outlined in my first book, *Stress-Free Money*, the goal of getting your financial house in order is to let go of that unnecessary stress and worry.

Our assessments leverage technology by testing over ten thousand potential scenarios in the future based on different relevant factors—interest rate changes, high or low inflation, variations in investment outcomes from high to negative, spending variability, tax considerations, and so on. We input all the "what ifs" that people worry about.

Financial technology programs are great for projecting your financial outcomes with a high probability of accuracy when you provide various inputs. As a result, you can see whether your current financial activities, behaviors, and habits will lead to success in attaining your goals. For instance, imagine you have $10 million invested, and your goal is to take out $600,000 a year to cover all of your expenses. Based on your debt, loans, taxes, and intended retirement age, we can tell you with very high probability the likelihood of success of your current financial plan. The algorithms and "Monte Carlo simulations" will calculate the range of potential scenarios across ten thousand iterations—good markets, bad markets, high-interest rates, low-interest rates, high inflation, low inflation—and determine your probability of success based on your financial numbers.

Most people don't actually know where they stand financially, even if they're exceptionally smart and successful, make lots of money, and have lots of money. Because they don't have that clarity, they carry unnecessary stress and anxiety about their financial situation. You can turn that stress into confidence once professionals have reviewed your situation and given you assessments based on real data. But if you never test it, you'll never know. Do your financial and health exams to know exactly where you are today and where you need to go.

By using technology, you can validate your concerns while also making accurate projections about how those concerns would play out, should they come to pass. You can model different scenarios for your financial future and plan accordingly. What if you sell their business, buy this property, invest a certain amount, spend a certain amount, or take out a new loan? You can leverage technology to test all the scenarios and then make well-informed decisions.

Sometimes, such an assessment is hugely stress-relieving because instead of needing to tighten their belt, clients learn they're investing plenty and already have access to more flexibility and freedom than they ever thought possible. They can finally take a deep breath and relax a bit. The non-financial spouse tends to sigh in relief at that news. Because there's hard evidence they're on track to reach their goals, the financially oriented spouse can calm down a bit, which brings more peace and harmony to the family.

The same is true for health. You might feel healthy but learn through in-depth assessments there are certain blood markers indicating potential for diseases and a need for changes in your lifestyle and diet. Maybe you're predisposed to certain cancers and can take proactive steps. Without that information, you're just walking around hoping things are okay.

Every day people (non-experts) have a limited capacity to assess and analyze their financial situation on their own, which leads them to get caught up in believing financial myths and making mistakes because of personal biases. Without expert help, you're likely to rely on the money blueprints from your parents, friends, or neighbors, which are often misguided and not applicable to you personally. As a result, you make decisions based on misinformation.

Technology doesn't necessarily tell you what's right or wrong, but queried correctly, it provides relevant, accurate data to inform your decision making. Pairing that technology with expertise and coaching to interpret the data allows you to make the right decision. My daughter McKinley is a Division 1 basketball player for Brigham Young University, now playing in the prestigious BIG 12 Conference. They've got a rigorous training schedule during the season, with early morning weightlifting, team practices, skills training, etc.

At this high level of athletics, they're using a lot of technology and data to help each player become better. Their physical trainers and nutritionists use the latest 3D body scanner technology to measure their body composition. Based on the data, coaches and trainers can give specific workout routines and nutrition advice. When she goes into the stadium late at night to shoot baskets for an hour or two, there is technology in the basketball, on her shoe, and dozens of cameras on the ceiling. Every single shot is tracked, measured, and reported to her coaches. They can give the percentage of shots taken and made from everywhere on the court, even measuring the arch of the ball in the air. This technology, combined with some of the top D-1 coaches in the country, gives her and her teammates a great competitive advantage to learn, make adjustments, and continue to become better basketball players. If you look at the NBA and other professional sports, technology and data analytics has completely changed everything.

 "Technology has the power to transform how we think, work, and live. Those who embrace it will have a significant advantage in the future."

— SATYA NADELLA // CEO OF MICROSOFT

VALUING AND LEVERAGING TECHNOLOGY

You now understand why it's important to look to the experts, and true experts will be up to date on the latest technology relevant in their field to benefit your health and wealth. We embrace technology at Pacific Capital, but this is not industry-specific, as seen by the example of my daughter and her college athletics. My personal trainer looks at my cloud-based food log, for instance, and he tracks my macronutrients—protein, fat, and carbohydrates—to give me better feedback and customize my meals to help me reach my goals. The percentage mix may change based on what our focus is for the month, but it would be impossible to get great results without technology and data analytics.

Successful people have key qualities in common when it comes to leveraging technology:

- **Adaptability**—They recognize the importance of being adaptable and willing to change with the times. They understand that new technology can be a powerful tool for achieving their goals and are willing to adapt to new tools and processes to stay competitive.
- **Innovation**—They are constantly looking for new ways to innovate and improve their businesses. They understand that new technology can help them do so by providing new solutions and approaches to old problems.
- **Efficiency**—They are always looking for ways to improve efficiency and productivity. They recognize that new technology can help them streamline their operations and get more done in less time.

- **Vision**—They have a clear vision of where they want to go and how they want to get there. They recognize that new technology can help them achieve their vision faster and more effectively.

- **Risk-taking**—They are not afraid to take risks and try new things. They understand that new technology can be risky, but also recognize that the potential rewards can be significant.

- **Learning**—They are lifelong learners. They understand that new technology requires ongoing learning and development, and they are willing to invest time and resources into learning new tools and processes.

- **Collaboration**—They value collaboration and teamwork, understanding that new technology can help them collaborate more effectively with others and achieve their goals faster and more efficiently.

- **Consideration of Others**—They are focused on their customers and clients and are always looking for ways to improve the experience and widen their impact. They recognize that new technology can help them personalize and streamline service to expand the reach of their work.

Technology plus expertise leads to the objective feedback you need to get better results. You may be good with technology and think you can use the apps or the tech without the coaching to go with it, but you bring your own story to it. Your personal bias (that you often aren't aware of) and your tendency to make excuses for yourself will be an obstacle to getting to the elite level you really could reach. For example, you might try a BMI assessment that indicates you're overweight, but it's tempting to say you're "big-boned," or it's your cousin's birthday weekend, so you need to make an exception and "live it up" for just this weekend. An objective expert will hold you accountable and the data analytics will not lie. If you're trying to reach specific goals, then there is black-and-white information about where you stand and what you need to do to get there. When my wife and I got home from a multi-week family trip to Europe, there was no hiding that I'd slipped up a bit. My trainer knew as soon as I logged in my weight and body fat stats when we returned to California. Was it kind of embarrassing? Of course it was. But the numbers were the numbers. At some point, we all need to face the cold, hard facts and avoid rationalizing and making excuses for why we aren't meeting our goals.

> "The Whoop Band, in particular, has been a game-changer for me in terms of helping me optimize my sleep. Every morning, it sends you a survey of activities you performed the night prior, such as 'Had a late meal,' 'took Melatonin,' 'wore blue light-blocking glasses,' etc. Then, at the end of each month, it tells you how each of your activities affected your sleep performance. Personally, I was fascinated to discover that wearing blue light-blocking glasses for three hours before bed improved my sleep effectiveness by thirteen percent... that's like getting around

thirty minutes of extra sleep! I would have never known that had I not utilized this technology to assess myself honestly."

— CRAIG CLEMENS // CO-FOUNDER OF
GOLDEN HIPPO

With technology alone, you can make some progress, but not as quickly or efficiently as if you pair technology with a coach or an expert. You might feel tempted to stop tracking your information, like how I felt when I returned home from Europe this summer, but if you're accountable to someone else, you'll mitigate the damage of going off track and be able to recover much quicker.

As the saying goes, what gets measured gets improved, and what gets measured and reported gets improved exponentially. That's why finding experts who can leverage these technologies objectively for your benefit is so important. The experts are paid to do this every day. They can introduce you to other technology, tools, and data that can get you results even faster than you previously thought possible. Because they're in this business, they are on the cutting edge of what's new and what's working for others like you.

For instance, a technology that came out in the financial industry a few years ago is the dynamic balance sheet, which aggregates all of your financial accounts, all cash flow, all investments, and all investment income into one clean dashboard. Instead of individually logging into your different bank and investment accounts to check your balances and transactions, we can create one login that allows you and your spouse and even your CPA or CFO to see all of your assets and liabilities in one place, organizing your important documents, summarizing your net worth, and the balances of your loans, assets, and investments, updated on a minute-by-minute basis. There's no longer a need to log in to ten different places and waste all that time; instead, there's one efficient financial dashboard for your family. For entrepreneurs with complex financial lives, it's an incredible time saver that allows you to zoom out and see the forest for the trees. A skilled wealth manager can introduce you to that technology and get it all set up for you.

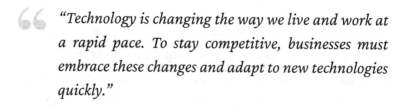

"Technology is changing the way we live and work at a rapid pace. To stay competitive, businesses must embrace these changes and adapt to new technologies quickly."

— JEFF BEZOS // FOUNDER & FORMER CEO OF
AMAZON

ARTIFICIAL INTELLIGENCE

I believe AI will change the world, business, and our lives so drastically that we won't even recognize what it used to be like. **Not embracing and figuring out how to best utilize AI is like living in another era and deciding not to learn how**

to use this new thing called the telephone or the automobile.

If you don't think our world is about to change, you're in for a shock. This technology can create PowerPoint presentations, summarize lengthy business contracts, and make up artistic logos from scratch in just a few seconds. Visionary entrepreneur and author of best-seller *Value Creation Kid,* Scott Donnell, is the primary founder of GravyStack–a kids' banking app for financial literacy–and I'm a co-founder.

He wanted to get fit and trim and lose twenty pounds. He asked ChatGPT to create a workout and diet plan to lose twenty pounds in less than three months. It created three months of fitness routines and provided specific meal plans for him: three meals a day for three months. He then asked the technology to give him the recipes and ingredients for all the meals and then a week-by-week grocery list to fulfill the meal plans for that ninety-day period. Then he had it organize everything into a calendar, spelling out *when* and *what* to eat and when and *how* to work out, day by day. His assistant now copies and pastes the grocery lists into his grocery store app to make weekly purchases, and the food shows up at his door.

All the planning and prep were done for him, and it took just a matter of minutes. How long would it have taken to contact a trainer, talk to a nutritionist, and figure out the meal plans and groceries by hand?

That's the power of technology. Don't shy away from AI. It's here to stay, and it's only getting faster and smarter. Leverage it and find experts who recognize the future and are leveraging it as well.

> "In today's fast-paced world, staying on top of new technologies is essential for success."
>
> — JACK MA // CO-FOUNDER OF ALIBABA GROUP

TECHNOLOGY AS A GOAL ACCELERATOR AND BRAINSTORMING PARTNER

Technology is a goal accelerator, so why would you avoid it just because it's unfamiliar? Even if you can't learn how to use it yourself, that's okay. Partner up with someone who understands it. Going back to Dan Sullivan's idea of "who, not how," you don't have to know how to do everything with technology. You just need to know who can help you utilize the technology.

Who can help you achieve your goal ten times faster?

Technology will help you know exactly where you stand and help efficiently create a plan for getting where you want to go... based on the numbers and not emotions. The key in leveraging technology is knowing the best prompts and questions to input. AI won't give you the answer you need unless you ask the right question. From there, you can use your strengths and interpretation to revise and adapt the information it aggregates.

For instance, I was doing my annual employee reviews, and I wanted to find ideas for ten thoughtful and insightful questions I could ask my team during our reviews. I wanted questions that would help me understand their goals, their challenges, and what makes them excited about working here. Because I specifically asked the technology to make these questions nontraditional and unexpected, the answers allowed team members to express themselves in a way that otherwise would have never happened. These were the most engaging and enlightening employee reviews we've ever had.

If you embrace technology, it will make you faster and better. It's a tool, not an obstacle. It doesn't replace you (but I believe those who use it well WILL replace you). Learning to evolve gives you a competitive advantage and helps you stay ahead of the curve. It's like walking across the country versus flying in a jet.

AI forces you to do things that matter and to use your gifts, creativity, and talents rather than just being an information processor and regurgitator, which is very low-value. It enhances rather than replaces creativity because it relieves you of the minutiae of administrative tasks or beginning templates from scratch. I've always advocated for delegating as much as possible besides your special gift(s), and AI is a tool to help you do that, allowing you the space to be more focused, fulfilled, relaxed, successful, and productive. Don't sleep on it.

> *"Technology is a key driver of innovation and growth. Businesses that invest in it will have a significant advantage in the marketplace."*

— INDRA NOOYI // FORMER CEO OF PEPSICO

The Oura Ring can also connect to other software such as Fitness Pal and my Superhuman app, where I keep track of my workouts and everything I eat... and it's not just me! I recently attended a conference and was in the company of other highly successful entrepreneurs early in the morning at the hotel's fitness center; I saw *all* of them looking at some version of an app for their workouts.

Reporting the tracked data to an expert coach is much more effective than simply typing something into a black hole with the intention to keep yourself accountable. Get someone else to help hold you accountable for your metrics and your results. (For example, knowing I have a weekly FaceTime call with my trainer makes me much more likely to stick to my plan.) As I make daily decisions, I'm aware I'll need to talk about them later, which deters me from making bad choices.

Using technology to track your data is a phenomenal first step. Using technology to track and report to accountability partners and coaches is even better. My results have been so good that now my wife wants input from my trainer on *her* diet and exercise. She's already in incredible shape, but she sees the value of continual improvement. I've had many people ask me what I did to get the results I've gotten, so I've made many referrals to the CEO Fitness Coaching group that I joined. What's most impressive to me is to see all of these referred friends and business clients of mine get the same results or even better results than I did! That validates that all of this works.

> "Wealth and fitness are decisions you make. How you get results is through accountability. I am fortunate to have a relationship with my wife for thirty years and the shared accountability that has come with growing up and building a family together. Our financial success and fitness as a couple has been a result of holding one another accountable."
>
> — CHRISTOPHER TURNER // FOUNDER OF EMERGICON, EMERGIFIRE, & EMERGIP

Some people in my circle are intensely into biohacking, and many of them do quarterly plasma replacements and invest in other age reversal treatments. They're always on the lookout for new ways to create health and energy and extend their healthy lifespan. Until you test with technology, you don't actually know where you stand and what you need to do.

"The two main hesitations people have about biohacking are that they think it requires expensive equipment and that it's not scientific.

Biohacking can be as simple as taking a cold shower or dimming the lights at night. The acts are intended to be simple bypasses around the interferences that we all face in our environments. Yes, I've invested fairly large sums of money in equipment, but still most of my 'bio hacks' are free or nearly free. You just have to do them.

The scientific rigors of the biohacking community run deep. The majority of individuals in this community rely on cutting-edge scientific data and then track their results. Biohacking was a term that was coined by Dave Asprey, a computer hacker who was looking for a way to optimize his health when he was obese. Just like any good computer programmer tests their hypothesis, so does a good biohacker measure their results. That's one of the core tenets of biohacking."

— REGAN ARCHIBALD, LAC, FMP // FOUNDER
OF EAST WEST HEALTH & PEPTIDE EXPERT

Using technology to get a real, deep, third-party, objective assessment not only makes you better—it allows you to see where you are relative to achieving your

goals. Based on your current circumstances, you can see whether you're on track and whether your goals are even possible. It's not about the power of positive thinking; it's about adjusting your behavior based on the real data.

When integrating technology into your health and wealth building, keep these principles in mind:

• Embrace technology; don't fear it. It will free up your time.

  – Assess how you're using technology to help you get to your goals right now. (Example: MyFitnessPal, Oura Ring, etc.)

  –Decide what tech will help you track the metrics you identified as most useful to your progress and goals in Chapter Three.

  – Utilize technology platforms that will aggregate all of your account balances in one place and give you your living balance sheet, cash flow, and other important financial updates all in one place.

  – Track your cash flow, keep data and analytics on any real estate investments you own, review the year-over-year changes in your cash flow and net worth

• Next-level health care and wealth care come from pairing experts with cutting-edge technological innovation.

  – Ask the experts what technology they personally use and would recommend.

– New technology for investment and financial management comes out every year. Talk to your wealth advisory team about what tech tools are out there that can make better wealth-building decisions.

"Success is a few simple disciplines, practiced every day; while failure is simply a few errors in judgment, repeated every day."

– JIM ROHN

5
LEVERAGE THE COMPOUND EFFECT

What do you think has a greater effect on cleaning your teeth and maintaining dental health—brushing for thirty minutes a week on Sunday morning, or brushing for two minutes in the morning and two minutes at night, seven days a week?

Similarly, is it better to work out one hour a day, seven days a week, or once a week for seven hours? In which case would you build more muscle and fitness?

Of course, the answer is obvious: regular, daily attention trumps periodic cramming sessions. These are silly examples, but the takeaway is clear and powerful: consistency in daily habits is essential and makes a greater long-term impact.

If your fitness trainer tells you to do seven hours of strength training and cardio per week, and you decide you're going to save it all until Saturday, working out for seven straight hours will have a significantly different impact than working out for an hour a day. Your body will feel monumentally different at the end of the week.

Now, project those two methods over a ten-year period. One person will have injuries and significant health issues, because they're essentially sedentary except for one overly intense day out of seven. The other will have built up strength, cardiovascular health, consistency, muscle foundation, and healthy habits.

 "Four years ago, I set a goal of making a million dollars. At the time, I was earning about $250,000 per year. I went to work on the mindset of money and the limitations I had unconsciously. For the first three quarters of the year, I kept the same $250,000 per year pace.

And then it happened. Even though I wasn't pacing a million dollars, I still held that goal in my mind daily. After a Q4 comeback, we ended the year at $987,000.

I didn't hit my yearly goal, but the next year we skipped a million and ended up at $3.5 million. The game doesn't have to be linear. If you stay consistent, you can make a quantum leap at any time."

— JOHN MADSEN // CEO OF SUPRA HUMAN

Financially, many entrepreneur investors take money from their business to pay themselves a bonus at the end of the year based on their profits. For example, if they make $3.5 million in profit, they'll take out $2.5 million at the end of the year to invest and leave the remainder for the business. That sounds like a good plan, but it's just like exercising for seven hours on Saturday.

Instead, at Pacific Capital, we encourage clients to set up weekly investment deposits from their checking account into their investment account. This cultivates consistency and allows for compound growth to do its magic. You get fifty-two chances to make new investments and plant new seeds of growth at different times throughout the economic cycle, which has fluctuations in interest rates, the stock market, and real estate. As a baseball analogy, it's like having fifty-two at-bats instead of one at-bat, giving you many more opportunities to get base hits and score runs.

 "My important daily habits are waking up and immediately getting out of bed and getting the day started. I want to start my run as soon as possible. No phone. No distractions. It's been a game-changer.

In fact, I run seven days a week—like clockwork. It's like meditation for me, both spiritual and physical, and it makes all the difference."

— COLE ZUCKER // ZUVI INVESTMENTS

It's natural to think of a goal and have a burst of motivation, but what matters more than that initial burst is regular follow-through.

I'm sure these examples make sense to you. What I've found, though, is even generally successful people who understand the principles have a harder time practicing them. As a result, you miss out on much of the potential compounding effect of small, regular habits that could benefit all areas of your health and wealth.

> *"Compound interest is the eighth wonder of the world. He who understands it, earns it... he who doesn't... pays it."*
>
> — ALBERT EINSTEIN

LONG-TERM THINKING

Make decisions today based on where you're headed in the long term. Be patient yet willing to pivot when necessary. Knowing your direction is better than speed.

> *"The obvious application of small, simple compounding habits applies to running one hundred miles. I didn't just go from running a few miles per day to running one hundred miles. I started with running three miles per day, four times per week. The next week, I ran the same amount but did five miles on my fourth run of the week. I incrementally built*

up my running body over a period of six months in SMALL amounts.

It was a long process, and a tedious one at times, but the end result was a physical body that was able to withstand thirty-four hours of running with no sleep. Looking back on it, I'm sure I could have gone two hundred miles, but my mind was focused on one hundred (hence the reason I 'hit the wall' at mile ninety-five). People tell me all the time that running is so boring and tedious. Or that the only time they'll run is if they're chasing a ball. I don't disagree with either of these statements, but for me I've found that DAILY physical activity of some sort is just as important for my PHYSICAL health as it is for my MENTAL health.

I joke with people that it's a lot cheaper to buy a new pair of running shoes each month than it is to see a psychiatrist or therapist each week. Regular physical activity is a must for me. It doesn't have to be running, pick any physical activity that makes you sweat and stick with it. Incremental gains lead to big results."

— ANONYMOUS ENTREPRENEUR

The highest achievers do the hard things daily, the hard things that don't show results for a really long time. That long-delayed gratification is inherently difficult, as we've discussed. You might know in your head, have heard, and believe this approach works, but it's still hard to keep going when you don't see results. Some results take months, and others take years. In the meantime, you're acting on faith that your effort will eventually pay off.

After one day of working out for an hour and then eating a healthy breakfast, a chicken salad at lunch, and some fish and vegetables at dinner, you're not instantly in peak shape and full of energy. Your blood tests and vitals don't change overnight.

Likewise, even if you save and invest money for a whole year, you may not see a significant difference in your net worth. Your investments might not grow or may even lose value in the first few months or first year. However, if you keep up the habit, you could be in a much better place financially after five to ten years.

These concepts are not new, and you might be nodding your head right now and saying, "I already know this." That's okay. The repetition of truth doesn't hurt us, so I'll say it again. The big difference between those who succeed at an elite level and those who don't is the consistent pursuit of habits despite not seeing immediate results. Overnight financial success stories aren't actually overnight successes; they usually have fifteen years of investing or working behind them.

"I try to be more stoic with my approach to money. I'm aggressive in general, (when it comes to money and investing) so the highs and lows can create some inner turmoil.

I've lost too much when I try to time the market. I'm playing the long game so I set it and forget it. I have automatic deductions from my checking account so I can systematically invest on a consistent basis."

— REMON KARIAN // FOUNDER OF
FIORELLA'S & ITALIAN RESTAURANT OWNER
IN THE NORTHEASTERN U.S.

THE CHINESE BAMBOO TREE

The best example of "overnight success" is the Chinese bamboo tree. It takes five years of planting, watering, and nurturing the soil to see a result. In the first through fourth years, there are no visible signs of change—no growth above the soil. The practice tests the patience of the gardener. Is the work to care for the tree worthwhile? What's the reward? Finally, in the fifth year, there's a miracle: the tree emerges above ground. Not only that, it grows *eighty feet in six weeks.*

So, nothing was happening before that exponential growth the fifth year? Wrong. Instead, the tree was growing, just underground where it wasn't as visible. It was developing a root system that could support that fifth-year surge (and beyond). In other words, the tree needed the foundation to sustain its healthy growth.

The same principle is true for people. People who patiently toil toward worthwhile dreams and goals build strong character while overcoming adversity and challenges as well as success. They have a strong internal foundation for both struggle and achievement.

Lottery winners, by contrast, are usually unable to sustain their unearned sudden wealth. Had the Chinese bamboo tree farmer dug up the little seed every year to see if it was growing, they would've stunted the Chinese bamboo tree's growth. As surely the caterpillar is doomed to a life on the ground, if it's freed from its struggle inside the cocoon prematurely. The struggle in the cocoon is what gives the future butterfly the wing power to fly, just as tension against the muscles as we exercise strengthens our muscles. Muscles left alone soon atrophy.

The Chinese bamboo tree is the perfect parable to our own experience with personal growth and transformational change. Of course, it's never easy and you won't see results for a long time. It's slow to show any progress. It's frustrating and unrewarding at times, but it's so worth it, especially if you can be patient and persistent.

When you're growing your root system beneath the ground, you're making progress, even though no one can see it—not even you.

Understanding the effects of habits, consistency and compound growth is so powerful because of that massive burst of eighty foot energy once you've laid the foundation. **On a linear graph, the line progresses evenly at forty-five degrees. On an exponential graph, it starts flatter but then reaches nearly vertical progress. You can harness that exponential growth for building both your health and your wealth if you can build on the habits in this book.**

Dr. Benjamin Hardy says you have to grow 10X internally before you can 10X externally. In other words, you have to become 10X better within yourself before you can grow 10X bigger or 10X more successful. Success starts on the inside, and the inside is the unseen. You build your internal foundation through habits and consistency.

You need the patience, long-term perspective, discipline, and willingness to stay the course, consistently doing what you say you're going to do, which is much harder than it seems. It's also extremely powerful. Small gains over time can have a big impact, just as a small seed can grow into a mighty tree.

 "Motivation is what gets you started. Habit is what keeps you going."

— JIM ROHN

WHEN TO PERSIST AND WHEN TO PIVOT

The value of consistency is clear, which also leads to another question: How do you know when it's time to pivot or to make a change? When should you lean into patience and keep going, and when is it time to reevaluate? Reevaluation most often comes from the experts on your team who are responsible for giving you feedback and advice.

If you seek regular feedback from the experts on your health and wealth team, they'll have informed advice ready for you about adjusting, pivoting, or making changes as needed. Most people don't have both a health and a wealth team; they tend to have one or the other, or just one expert they look to who can't actually cover all the bases. To achieve next-level success, you need bona fide teams in both areas, with the knowledge that health and wealth work in tandem.

If you don't have a trusted, vetted team, and you're trying to do it all on your own, you might make excuses or you'll settle for less than your best, thinking your progress is "good enough already." You'll be tempted to give yourself an out and quit when the going gets tough. But a team will help steer you on the best possible course and keep you motivated, informed, and encouraged all along the way. If you're making a poor decision—like liquidating to invest your whole net worth in crypto, for example—an expert will intervene so you don't work against yourself. I use this as an example because

I had to save someone from making that exact mistake last year.

There's a saying that you shouldn't be your own pilot and your own surgeon. The same is true for being your own health coach and your own wealth manager. These issues are too important to take into your own hands. You need objective, third-party experts to help you course-correct when necessary and to tell you the truth when you won't tell yourself the truth.

Quite a few of our clients at Pacific Capital have been tempted to change investments based on something they read in a magazine or saw in an online article. I've often asked, "If you read a magazine article about how to perform an appendectomy, would you feel tempted to buy the surgical instruments on Amazon and try it on yourself?" No, of course not. So with that same sound reasoning, let the health and wealth experts guide your strategy.

 "We are what we repeatedly do. Excellence, then, is not an act, but a habit."

— ARISTOTLE

THE IMPORTANCE OF MINDSET

A positive mindset is essential for creating both optimal health and abundant wealth. These both involve having a growth-oriented perspective, focusing on what's possible, overcoming your limiting beliefs, and embracing challenges in your journey as opportunities for growth. These principles sound simple, but they're not easy.

There will be setbacks, recessions, investment market downturns, business struggles, health challenges, doctor's visits, and unexpected emergencies that keep you from eating healthier and exercising consistently. You must have a resilient mindset that allows you to bounce back if you're going to succeed.

If you look to the future and think it will be easy just because you hire experts, I have bad news for you. It's still gonna be hard. Many setbacks are outside your control, so just assume you'll get knocked off course; in those moments, remember your why, and get yourself back on track as quickly as possible.

When my friend fell off the fitness wagon, he stayed on the ground until he got new encouragement. Who knows how long he would've stayed there if he and I didn't happen to have that conversation? When you get knocked down in a boxing match, you need to decide whether you'll stand back up or stay down for the count. Only one of those choices leads to success.

One of my favorite books is *The Compound Effect* by Darren Hardy. He writes, "You will never change your life until you change something you do daily. The secret of your success is found in your daily routines."

"The secret of your success is found in your daily routine."

— JOHN C. MAXWELL

PRIORITIZING AND RECHARGING

If you're reading this book, you're probably a busy professional with a million and one demands already begging for your attention. You lead people who need you to meet with them and train them, you likely have a family to care for, you've got other people in your industry clamoring for your time, and more. Simply knowing you should invest in your health and wealth isn't the same as carving out the space and attention to make it happen.

You can't pour anything from an empty cup. And if I know you like I think I do, many people depend on you. If you're depleted, you've got nothing to offer them. You're likely the person others rely on for support, and look up to for guidance in your circles. So you need an abundance of health and wealth of your own to continue supporting everyone around you.

You are who you are because you've achieved great things in your past. But you can't recharge others if you've got no energy to start with. It takes resources to do all the great things that you do. That's one reason it's essential to create peak wealth and peak health to fulfill the mission that you're here on earth to fulfill. As author and speaker Simon Sinek says, "I know I have to look after myself, and I know I have to take care of myself. I have no problem turning things down that are for money [if they conflict with those]."[1]

Taking care of yourself and ensuring you're not overstressed will safeguard your mental health, too. I prioritize many self-care practices so I can show up for myself and all the people who need me. I journal regularly, engage in prayer and meditation, get massages, practice deep breathing, and find ways to destress and avoid overwhelm. I take time away from all my screens to get out in nature. My favorite place to escape stress is out in the ocean. Riding waves and immersing myself in the salty ocean water has always been a way to refresh and reset myself mentally. I also love to physically handwrite in my journal outdoors, far away from any digital devices; I'll write about what I'm grateful for and goals or ideas I'm working on.

Never tried it? You should! Research suggests strong benefits in physically connecting the brain and the hands through writing with a pen and paper. It allows you to get deeper into your subconscious, both to uncover new ideas and to root new habits, than if you type or dictate into your phone. In general, I'm a very digital person, but I keep a physical journal for this purpose. I use it to clear thoughts from my head every single day and make room for new ideas. Getting your thoughts on paper cultivates a lot of mental clarity.

Learning to relax and recharge has been another important process for me. As a growth-focused entrepreneur, I feel a constant urgency to achieve more. Maybe it's being the oldest child, somewhat of a Type-A personality. In the past, relaxation often felt like a waste of time—I felt like I was being unproductive. The constant mode of doing and achieving more has served me well to a point, but it becomes counterproductive if I push myself towards burnout or exhaustion. It's hard for me even to sit through a movie sometimes because it feels like I could be more productive doing something else.

Over time, though, I've become self-aware that constant productivity is not healthy. As I've gained that clarity, I've thought about what could help me completely disconnect, detach, and slow down. I still need help in those areas. **People like us often don't have the ability to relax and let go. It's just not in our DNA. We're always going from one scheduled event to the next, and even "down time" ends up being some sort of productive endeavor or connection-building interaction.**

We thrive on constant high pressure and lots of action, but the truth is, if we can take time to decompress and recharge, we'll achieve even more. When I'm less stressed and taking better care of myself, I'm in a better position to achieve and to serve others.

Benefit from the compounding effect of rest by building in and choosing rest on a regular basis, rather than building up pressure until you're forced to rest through illness. When we stop thinking about resting and recharging as unproductive and start realizing it's part of being *more* productive, we can trick ourselves into

accepting that challenge and applying the same discipline we would to other work. How can we build sufficient discipline to get quality sleep for seven and a half to eight hours a night? If we're used to working until 1 a.m., we'll need to get to bed earlier.

The compounding effect of rest, journaling, meditation, massages, and other self-care practices to keep your body and mind fresh is incredible. One of my favorite stories is about Bob Hope, who got at least a one-hour therapeutic massage, every day, seven days a week, for sixty-three years. He credited that practice with allowing him to live fifty percent beyond his life expectancy. He lived past a hundred, which was largely unheard of for his generation. The circulation in his body and the destressing of his mind strengthened his immune system. So much disease originates from internal blockages, which he prevented.

The compounding effect of rest and self-care also contributes to lifestyle freedom. When you keep your body and mind fresh, you're able to do more that brings you joy and adds value to the world via your Unique Ability®. Self-care activates other positive, productive aspects of your life. It's not a sacrifice of impact but an amplifier.

Rest is an investment. Making that investment allows you to be who you were called to be and to give your best self to the world, making your greatest impact and contribution. Your vitality, energy, and health are critical to performing as your best self.

"The greatest shortcoming of the human race is our inability to understand the exponential function."

— ALBERT BARTLETT

CULTIVATING BREAKTHROUGH HABITS

The principle of the compound effect is a key strategy for success in both the pursuit of optimal health and significant wealth. The compound effect is all about making small, consistent changes over time that can lead to big results. **By focusing on daily habits and routines, you can create powerful momentum that will carry you towards your health and fitness goals over time. Whether it's committing to a daily workout routine or making small changes to your diet, every small step you take will add up to big improvements in your overall health and well-being.**

In the arena of wealth, while I suggest investing weekly, I do not suggest checking your investment account balances weekly. Checking on your investments frequently has the opposite effect you would expect. Because market volatility leads people to feel fear, it also causes people to make very bad decisions. They get the illusion that they can control their investments or perfectly time the market, but in reality, the portfolio growth should be more like the Chinese bamboo tree discussed earlier in this book. Don't keep digging it up to check whether it's growing, or you'll just kill it altogether. It might take ten years of nurturing to see the growth you really want, and in the meantime, you need consistency and patience.

The best habit is to just avoid the temptation to over monitor the ever-changing value of your investments. (See, all of these habits overlap for a reason!) Trust that in the long run it will grow like that tree, eighty feet in six weeks, but in the shorter run, your job is simply to water and care for the roots. It's hard to have that faith.

Even my clients with $25 million to $50 million saved up struggle with this practice. When the markets get scary for them, many (not all) of them still have the same temptations to bail and change course. Some even obsessively log in to see their balances and then want to know what they can do, what they can change. They figure they have to change something to weather the storm, instead of trusting they've built the right foundation to withstand it already. The bamboo may already be emerging, but they suddenly want to prune it instead of feeding it. In times of turmoil, trust the farmer— trust the expert.

Against your natural instincts, stop checking and rechecking. Those moment-by-moment updates aren't what you need. They're not in your control anyway. What *is* in your control is finding ways to earn money and investing the highest percentage you possibly can, frequently, rain or shine. Don't turn your automated weekly investment contributions off just because it's stormy outside. Keep planting seeds for future trees to grow. In fact, the ones that you plant during stormy times will likely grow into the biggest trees. When the economy looks frightening, that's often the best time to plant.

Education is another habit that compounds over time. It's critical for achieving both health and wealth goals. It's important to learn about healthy habits and financial management strategies in order to make informed decisions and set clear, specific goals that will give you direction and motivation. These practices help you make and track progress over time.

 "We first make our habits, and then our habits make us."

— JOHN DRYDEN

One of the key benefits of the compound effect is that it highlights the importance of consistency in achieving long-term results. Rather than trying to make drastic changes all at once, focus on developing sustainable habits that you can maintain over time. By building positive health habits into your daily routine, you can create a powerful momentum that will carry you towards your goals and keep you on track even when things get tough.

Try these tips:

• Pick one specific, measurable habit for health care and another for wealth care that are each achievable daily and that will yield big dividends over time.

    – Pick habits to stack that will act as a domino effect, as discussed in *Tiny Habits: The Small Changes That Change Everything* by Dr. BJ Fogg.

EXAMPLE OF HABIT STACKING

HEALTH: Putting floss next to the toothpaste

WEALTH: Auto-contributing each paycheck into an investment account

— Read *The Compound Effect* by Darren Hardy.

> ### EXAMPLE OF THE COMPOUND EFFECT
>
> If real estate markets have completely dropped, consider a pivot of taking money from your bond investments and buying distressed real estate.

• Focus on consistency and discipline. Motivation is unreliable, but habits will carry you through.

   — Decide your daily must-do's. Pick at least one habit for fitness and health and one for financial wealth, to start. These should be non-negotiables that you've chosen to implement because of this book.

• Talk to your chosen experts about the best path for your health and wealth. Let them worry about the course while you apply yourself wholly to the effort.

   — Follow the coaching strategy of your experts *to a tee* for at least six months to see results.

"Excuses are the enemy of excellence."

– BOB PROCTOR

6

CUT THE EXCUSES

It's time for some tough love: you can have excuses or results, but not both. This chapter is about removing the blame and excuses from your life and telling yourself the truth about yourself. You have to be accountable to reach your "next-level self."

Taking ownership is about relinquishing excuses and admitting the results are up to you. Remove the blame and excuses from your life and say, "It's time for me to own this." No one can exercise for you. You have to take action yourself. Similarly, no one can up-level your investment savings each month. Only you can do that.

Think back to my introduction story in Denver, Colorado. The night after I started writing this book and embarking on this fitness journey, I attended a private dinner event at Ruth's Chris in downtown Denver. They had a special guest speaker, whose speech brought the entire crowd to their feet. Her name is Kirstie Ennis, a former U.S. Marine Corps sergeant who was injured in a helicopter accident in Afghanistan in 2012 and lost her left leg. Her stories of fighting in the war in Afghanistan was only part of her story. She showed pictures of her wounded leg before the amputation and told of the pain and recovery process after she returned home to the U.S.

Instead of sitting around gathering sympathy for her sacrifice and permanent disabilities, she decided to set some ridiculously ambitious goals and then went on and conquered them. Kirstie, on one leg, has now scaled six of the so-called

"Seven Summits"—the highest peaks on each of the seven continents! And she's not done yet. In her words, "I want to be the first amputee or above-the-knee amputee to swim the English Channel. I also want to do the Great Divide ride, which is a 2,600-mile transcontinental mountain bike ride. So, essentially Canada to Mexico. And then I want to do seven marathons, seven continents in seven days for the World Marathon Challenge." It was a pleasure to meet her and feel her energy and resilience. Kirstie embodies every concept taught in this book.

Now that you understand ridiculous ambition, avoiding temptation, looking to the experts, embracing new technology, and leveraging the compounding effect, you have to take action on what you've learned. You can know everything there is to know on this topic, but if you don't implement and execute, then all that knowledge is useless. Wisdom is *applied* knowledge.

It's one thing to have knowledge; it's another thing to have wisdom. Wisdom comes through action and experience. You only grow and get better once you begin taking action. Done is better than perfect.

Get started today, be accountable, and get your team in place to support you. Stop making excuses, because you *can* improve, no matter what your circumstances are today. There are no finish lines, so no matter where you are, you're not "already there." Success is all about reaching new and better milestones of progress that you pass along the way.

My favorite athlete-turned-business person is Shaquille O'Neal. He owns many different businesses and franchises. Whereas some athletes may rely on their agents to handle everything or throw in the towel after their playing days are over, Shaq took (and continues to take) control of his finances and future without making excuses or slowing down.

> "I try my best not to slip up, but admittedly I do. When this happens, I do a couple things: First, I weigh myself every single day, if only to immediately bring the focus back to my habits and also commitments to myself. It brings me to a point where I have no choice but to question my habits the day prior if what I see on the scale is not what I would expect. Secondly, I have goals I intend to knock out, written on neon-colored index cards that are strategically placed on a bulletin board above my desk in my office. Looking at my monitor daily, I cannot help but notice these couple of cards, keeping me accountable to my commitments."

— MIKE WEINER // FOUNDER OF
DISTINCTIVE DESIGNS 21, INC.

LEVELING UP

To level up, you need to let go of the mindset that says if you have $X million in your accounts, you're done—done growing, done being useful, done producing, done creating. Or if you reach a certain weight, you're healthy and don't have to exercise or watch what you eat anymore.

Those attitudes don't make sense, because when you stop tending to your health and wealth, you go backwards. When you reach a mountaintop, don't stop; instead, pick a new peak and start climbing toward it.

> *"My life is dedicated to solving the puzzle of 'What Creates Health?' and to figure out what interventions work in whom, at what time, and in what dose to create that individualized health. My progress towards this goal is deeply determined by my own physical and mental thriving. My health enables my good functioning which enables the good functioning of my patients."*
>
> — DAVID HAASE, MD // FOUNDER & CEO OF MAXWELL CLINIC; CMO OF YOUTOPIA

Continually look to improve, starting from where you are. Everyone starts in a different place, with different challenges, family dynamics, genetics, health backgrounds, financial experiences, and financial opportunities. It does not matter. Start anyway, instead of giving yourself excuses.

> *"Don't expect to be motivated every day to get out there and make things happen. You won't be. Don't count on motivation. Count on discipline."*

> — JOCKO WILLINK // AUTHOR & PODCASTER;
> FORMER U.S. NAVY OFFICER

It's time to take accountability for where you are today as a result of all the choices you've made in the past. Go back to Chapter One and set one or two ridiculously ambitious goals, whether you think you can reach them or not. There are no finish lines. Remember, it's really about the person you become in the process of pursuing those ridiculously ambitious goals.

In my other books, I've discussed how retirement doesn't really exist for people like us. We're people who will always want to stay in the game, remain useful ("retirement" literally means to take out of use) and keep growing. Which way will you grow? Whatever you choose is no accident, so choose growing toward greater health and wealth.

This extreme level of ownership requires a growth mindset. We all know what this means: taking accountability for your circumstances, viewing challenges and setbacks as opportunities for growth, and embracing continuous improvement. Knowing what it means and *doing it* are two different things. These qualities come more naturally to some of us than others, but the good news is, everything can be built. I believe in nurture over nature. We all come with unique gifts, talents, and tendencies, but so much of success comes from developable skills. Discipline is a skill that can be learned, as is evidenced by so many great leaders.

The bottom line is that you can only make transformational progress in your life and achieve the results you desire once you decide it's all up to you, at the end of the day. You have the power to make choices that will impact your life, and by taking accountability for your circumstances and results, you can create the positive change you want to see.

 "Excuses are a killer of progress. Whenever I catch myself making excuses, I know that I'm lacking commitment and the drive that's essential for achieving greatness. If I'm pursuing a transformational goal, something that will have a profound impact on my life, I know that making excuses is not an option.

To get back on track, I take a hard look at my priorities and goals. I ask myself whether the objective I'm working towards still aligns with my overall vision and if it's something I truly want to achieve. If I realize that the goal is still important and worth pursuing, I renew my commitment by developing a detailed action plan and breaking it down into smaller, more achievable milestones.

I remind myself of the reasons why I set the goal in the first place and visualize the impact achieving it will have on my life. I take time to focus on my mind-

set, and to confront my fears head-on. I refuse to let them hold me back, and instead, I take massive action to move myself forward.

Ultimately, progress demands discipline, and discipline means doing what needs to be done, even when I don't feel like doing it (motivation is irrelevant). I stay focused and keep pushing forward, no matter what. When it comes to achieving greatness, there are no shortcuts or excuses. It's all about taking consistent, relentless action towards my goals, and never settling for less than I'm capable of achieving."

— MICHAEL MOGILL // FOUNDER & CEO OF
CRISP

WHAT ABOUT PROCRASTINATION?

In my meetings with Dan Sullivan, we often talk about procrastination because Dan says procrastination is a gift. He says it's a sign that you need a different person to help you get something done that has kept you stuck. There's nothing wrong with it, according to Dan. You procrastinate because you're reaching for a goal that you don't personally have the capability to achieve on your own, and you don't have the support system in place yet to get that done and lift you to that next level.

His philosophy has completely changed my mind about procrastination. It's healthy if you take it as a signal that you're trying to do something you either don't know how to do or don't love doing. Good for you for trying; now, find the right person to do it moving forward. It's that simple.

Procrastination is a signal to your brain that says, "I need someone or something to help me, because I don't know how to do this on my own."

 "Success is not final, failure is not fatal: it is the courage to continue that counts."

— WINSTON CHURCHILL

Sometimes the work can't be outsourced, but it's still hard, and that's okay. Every week there are tasks that require some level of struggle.

You need to look your struggles right into the face. You need to understand, and constantly remain aware, of how difficult things are going to be. And you will have to accept the fact that you will struggle. Once you've done that, everything will become possible. Because you will no longer complain about how difficult things are. Because you are going to focus on doing the best work you possibly can.

 "Once all struggle is grasped, miracles are possible."

— MAO ZEDONG

Recently I traveled to two cities on the same day, arrived at a conference later than expected, went to the welcome dinner event, met a lot of great people, and caught up on a couple of phone calls. By the time I got to my hotel room, it was 11:45 at night. I had not done the weightlifting and cardio workout that I'd committed to doing every day.

I started bargaining with myself: maybe I'd just add an extra half hour to my workout the next morning. I really, really wanted to go to sleep. I was exhausted. Everything inside me said, *Just go to sleep. You don't need to work out.*

However, I'm all in and have systems to hold me accountable. This was not my scheduled rest day; that recovery period with no workout was scheduled to come two days later. I didn't want to log in my exercise app that I'd accomplished nothing for the day. I just couldn't do it. I have goals, I have a coach, and I need to practice what I preach.

So I changed into my fitness clothes and walked down to the fitness center just after midnight, and I worked out until 1:30 in the morning. I sent a video to my trainer, logged in my workout, and went to bed. Keeping that commitment to myself added to my already solid confidence. I can count on myself to follow through, be resilient, and find ways to prevail even when circumstances try to get in the way. Was I exhausted when my face hit that pillow? Absolutely. But I felt great, knowing I didn't settle for excuses.

Everyone keeps their discipline when they feel motivated. The difference between the high achievers and everyone

else is what they do when they *don't* feel motivated. It's easy to do big, great things when you feel like it; the real achievers do those big, great things even when they don't feel like it.

Do what you're supposed to do, even—or especially—when you don't feel like it. That's the essence of success. Push through.

 "If you want to change the world, you have to change yourself first."

— MAHATMA GANDHI

When people make big financial mistakes, they often want to blame others. "Well, my brother-in-law told me about that investment, and it was bad," they'll say. Or, "The real estate market changed, and interest rates went up." There are a million variations of "It wasn't my fault."

People have no shortage of financial excuses. They blame the government, the economy, their business partner, their employer, their investment advisor, etc. Ultimately, you build financial wealth through the decisions you make, so you have to take ultimate accountability for your financial circumstances. Success or failure is on you, not everyone else.

You can do everything I've talked about up to this point: set big goals, surround yourself with experts, use technology for data and tracking, and all the rest. They are ingredients for success, but you have to start by taking responsibility for where you are physically and financially.

Have you not been honest with yourself about where you are and how you got there, financially and health-wise? If so, that changes now!

 "It is not the strongest of the species that survives, nor the most intelligent, but the one most responsive to change."

— CHARLES DARWIN

When you start fully focusing and truly committing, you stop making up stories as to why you can't achieve your goals, and you stop ceding your control to others by blaming them. You already know these principles, but they're worth repeating. **After all, these steps to elite levels of success are relatively simple to understand but not at all easy to implement. If they were easy, everyone would do them.**

No excuses. The only one who can do your push-ups is you. Keep in mind:

• Whatever you're doing, give it your full attention. It's more effective to go all in with work and then all in with rest than to muddle between the two.

   – For one week, try single-tasking and time blocking (2–3 hour time blocks of focused activity). Concentrate on what you're doing with no phone and no distractions to pull your attention away.

   – Read or listen to the book *Deep Work* by Cal Newport.

• Adopt a mindset of personal responsibility. The buck stops with you.

   – Stop making excuses for yourself, starting today.

• If you find yourself procrastinating, it's a signal that you need to find a better person or resource to help with that task.

– If you are struggling to make a breakthrough, it's because you don't have the right resources, coaches, people, technology, guides, systems, and/or habits. Go outside yourself to avoid the yo-yoing up and down.

"The true meaning of life is to plant trees, under whose shade you do not expect to sit."

– NELSON HENDERSON

7
FORTIFY YOUR LEGACY

My friend Mark Corser is from Birmingham, a small town in England. He moved to California for work, and he was renting a house about five minutes away from my family. He came to our church to connect with the community, and we became friends.

His wife got pregnant with her second child, and he got laid off from his sales job. The company was based in the UK, and he couldn't find another job. His former boss back in the UK wasn't kind to him and tried to get him kicked out of the U.S. by telling the British embassy that his work visa had expired and he'd lost his job. By that point, his wife was seven and a half months pregnant and very sick. They could not safely fly back to their home country. He didn't know what to do, either financially or regarding his immigration status.

One of our mutual friends is an immigration attorney and started helping him figure out a solution. Mark worked in machinery sales and had been making cold calls to clients of one of the manufacturers who could potentially buy the machines he was selling. When he was down to a few thousand dollars left in his bank account and his wife was approaching her delivery date, he got a call back in the middle of the night from a potential client he had called eight months earlier.

"Hey, I've thought about it, and the timing is right. We want to buy one of those big machines."

Great news, right?

Unfortunately, my friend Mark had to say, "Oh, I'm sorry, I don't work for the company anymore. I got laid off."

The client suggested he call the manufacturer and see if he could still help them, because they specifically wanted to work with *him*. So Mark called the manufacturer, who said yes. A complete miracle! He closed a monumental sale that allowed his family to afford their rent to stay in the US, which gave him another idea: working for himself selling these machines to large U.S. companies! He created his own small business and was able to get his work visa sorted. Mark became so successful that he fulfilled his childhood dream of owning horses and building a beautiful farm home for his family. He left my neighborhood in Southern California and moved to Kentucky, where he now owns three hundred acres with dozens of racehorses for the Kentucky Derby. He and his wife had more kids, and my daughter and I visited him when she had a basketball tournament in that area.

He now lives on a farm among rolling, grassy hills that remind him of England. He went from growing up poor, to nearly getting deported, to breaking the cycle of poverty and building a different legacy for his family through consistently good financial habits. When it looked like nothing was going his way, he took a big chance. Now he's well known in the world of horse racing, living his dream, and helping the people he loves thrive. He has tons of employees both on the farm and in his machine manufacturing and sales business.

He went from absolute rock-bottom challenges in a new country to building an amazing legacy of wealth and tradition for his family, beyond what he could have dreamed of as a kid. When we visited their farm in Kentucky, my daughter and I could tell that he was so excited and proud of what he'd created for his family. This was exactly where he belonged.

Mark is an example of what building a family legacy from nothing can look like. What will yours look like?

> "I have an amazing wife of thirty years, eleven children (four of them married), eight grandchildren so far, and a calling on my life to build up people in the areas that matter most in life: faith, marriage, parenting, health, and value creation. All of this requires high-level energy and abundant resources! Life and business is an energy game.

Everything impacts energy! Your relationships, your time, your money, your attention, your thoughts, your diet, your exercise... everything!"

— CHAD JOHNSON // FOUNDER OF
G5SUMMIT.COM

MAKING AN IMPACT

If you're reading this, you've reached a level of success and wealth where you're no longer just living to make money. You can turn your attention from stressing about how to pay your bills toward creating a lasting impact and legacy. Maybe you want to know how many people you can help, like feeding one million children. Or maybe your goal is not as quantifiable, but you want to make a difference that at least outlives you. You want the world to be different because you exist.

When I was ten years old, I was having a hard time with my history homework. My dad loves to study history and knows everything about it. It's just his thing. I'm more of a futurist. I don't look to the past as much, and history was my hardest subject because I just couldn't get excited about it as a kid. My parents were harping on me for my history grade and wanting me to get better in the subject. Why wasn't I studying more?

Finally I blurted out, "I don't want to study history—I want to make history!" We laugh about it now, because it seemed like a ridiculous statement for a ten-year-old kid to make.

Years later, they told me I always thought much bigger about what was possible than they did. Now, as a father in my forties, I see I've always had the goal to make a big and lasting impact. It's exciting to do work that changes the world for the better, helping people in a way that their own family legacies will be transformed, and my contribution will have made a difference.

You could say I've always been ridiculously ambitious. Some people still need to develop that high ambition. The more you lean into your unique gifts and talents, the more you will serve the world, the greater and longer lasting your impact will be. You're already great at something and your community and the world needs more of it.

> "To be honest, I am not out to be a legend in terms of being wealthy... I am out to be legendary in how I manage my daily life and give back to my community. I enjoy impacting others with our ability to serve in a volunteer role and to support them financially. That, to me, is true abundant wealth."
>
> — MIKE WEINER // FOUNDER OF
> DISTINCTIVE DESIGNS 21, INC.

As author Joyce Meyer puts it, "The greatest gift you can give your family and the world is a healthy you."

When you make good choices around health and wealth, you set an example for your family members, particularly

your children. They're more likely to follow your foot-steps and adopt good habits that will benefit them for years to come.

We have a two-car garage that we converted into a gym, so we exercise at home instead of driving to a gym. Our five kids are currently ages seven to eighteen. On our kids' list of daily activities, exercise is always one of them. They also each play at least two sports at a competitive level, primarily basket-ball, volleyball, and football.

Like many, our kids love to be wherever their mom is. If she's in the kitchen, they hang out with her there. If she's upstairs in our bedroom, they want to hang out there. The number one question I get asked at home is "Where's Mom?" And often, Mom is in our garage gym exercising.

We have a rule that if you're in the gym, you're exercising. Our kids don't have the option to take an iPad into the gym and chill. That means if the kids want to hang out with their mom and she's in the gym, they put on their workout clothes and get on the treadmill, the Peloton bike, or the Stairmaster machine. After their workout, our kids always feel proud to tell us what they accomplished in the gym, whether it's running at a certain number of miles per hour or jumping rope for a certain number of times in a row. The more they accomplish, the more they look to us for what they should do next, which exhibits a growth mindset. Exercise begets more exercise. Each workout they do encourages them to do their next workout.

If my wife was not working out in our gym, but instead eating a bag of Cheetos and sitting on the couch watching TV for two hours, they'd follow that example too. **More is caught than taught. Kids follow what they see more than they obey empty words. "Do what I say, not what I do" doesn't work when you're talking about establishing your family legacy.**

Caring about our health and fitness is already having a great impact on the way our kids see themselves. They emulate what we do, and in our family, we prioritize healthy habits.

When we go on vacations, we pack our exercise clothes and workout together at the hotel fitness centers. Our health priorities have become theirs, in a way that will serve them their whole lives.

A healthy lifestyle can help reduce the risk of various health conditions, such as heart disease, diabetes, and obesity, in yourself and the family members who emulate you. You can also pass on your knowledge about healthy living, promoting health and wellness in your descendants.

Overall, transforming your personal health and fitness can have a profound impact on your family, empowering them to be their best selves and inspiring them to live life to the fullest. By prioritizing your health, you can create a lasting legacy of wellness and vitality that will endure for generations to come.

> "Your legacy is being written by yourself. Make the right decisions."
>
> — GARY VAYNERCHUK

Living a healthy lifestyle can have a significant impact on your family's emotional and social well-being as well. When you have confidence, feel good about your body, and follow the right nutrition, you have a higher capacity for joy, which contributes to mental health and helps your kids and everyone around you be happier.

Having exposure to sunlight, getting exercise, staying hydrated, and eating cleaner, single-ingredient foods benefits mental health. A large number of studies tout these benefits, which matter so much more today because children are spending ten times as much time on screens than kids did a decade ago. Most kids are indoors all the time, not getting regular sunlight, and not moving or exercising as much. They're sedentary much more of the time. It's no wonder we're seeing such a profound increase in childhood obesity, a mental health crisis, and an increase in violence, particularly since so much of the content on screens is violent, provocative, and negative. There's also pervasive bullying. These forces combine to create a decrease in mental, physical, and emotional health. But with awareness, education, and concerted efforts, we can certainly pave the way for a brighter, healthier future for our kids.

 "The best way to predict the future is to create it."

— PETER DRUCKER

STRENGTHENING FAMILY BONDS

Something as simple as grocery shopping and cooking together are opportunities for connection. In fact, there are so many opportunities for connection that we can miss if we aren't paying attention. My friends Jim and Jamie Shelis run a program called 18 Summers that reminds us that we only get that many summers with our kids before they're grown and offers a framework for making the most of that time. (If this concept speaks to you, I highly recommend their book, *The Family Board Meeting*.)

My family goes on evening walks or afternoon hikes together on Sundays. We get out in nature with no distractions. The seven of us exercise together and take in some fresh air on a day when there's no school, no sports, no homework, and no business. The kids open up and talk and share more when we're outdoors and in motion. When we ask them questions, they give us longer answers than if we were just sitting at home. This has turned out to bond us together while keeping us doing something healthy and active at the same time.

Nutritionally, our commitment to health is very influential on the kids. Think about life as a kid: you only eat what's available in front of you. Parents decide the health opportunities for children through what goes in the fridge and the pantry, which is both a responsibility and an opportunity. You can model healthy choices and contribute to their future rather than seeing the responsibility as a chore.

As parents, you can set a positive or a negative example. I've told my kids their bodies are a temple and need to be treated as such. You can teach your family to respect and honor their bodies. Teach them it's a privilege to eat and fuel yourself. Eating is not first and foremost about what tastes good but what gives you energy and makes you feel happy in the long run.

Of course, you can have treats, and so can they, but be mindful of the habits and patterns you teach them. If you teach your kids to eat sugar or junk food to cope with their emotions and struggles, that subconscious will be difficult to break as an adult. So be intentional.

Family health starts with what you eat, and my kids have internalized that message. In fact, at eleven years old, my son decided to go on a no-sugar, no-dessert, no candy diet for a full year to get back in great physical shape before his next football season. When he came to me with the idea, I offered him $1,000 as a reward. Shockingly he stuck to his goal the entire year, even on his birthday, Christmas, and Halloween. He earned that $1,000 reward and was so proud of himself! I wrote a LinkedIn post about it and included a picture of him holding ten $100 bills. He gained a lot of confidence in his own discipline, and he got healthier. The next year, three of the other kids wanted to try it.

During that year, he was absolutely tempted all of the time. Even his friend's mom who carpooled with him tried to get him to cheat. She said they were going to the donut shop to celebrate the end of the school term, and it wasn't a big deal if he had just one donut. She said she wouldn't tell anyone. Later she called and told us how strong and committed he was to this goal. He still had six months to go, and he said there was no way he'd break his streak. I'm convinced with his discipline and physical gifts, he'll be a famous athlete one day. We'll see!

CREATING A BETTER FUTURE

By creating abundant wealth in your family, you can provide your children and future generations with the means to support themselves and do good in their communities. In my previous book *Smart, Not Spoiled*, I talked about teaching kids good financial sense from early on. You have the opportunity to teach your kids that health and wealth go hand in hand and build from small, consistent habits.

As a legacy move, teach kids about financial management. Money management skills don't come from having money; they come from learning money management skills. Plenty of people think if you get more money, you'll suddenly get smarter about it, but that's false. Look no further than the hundreds of professional athletes and celebrities who come into wealth and then blow it all. Many end up bankrupt and have tax liens and debts they can't pay. Being fit for wealth includes both physical and mental fitness for wealth. It's important to prepare yourself and your loved ones to handle success.

You'll never receive more success than you can handle. If you do, you'll quickly blow it.

Being fit for wealth and helping your family to do the same has countless benefits for future generations:

- You leave a lasting mark on the world and provide them with the means to do the same, whether through philanthropy, entrepreneurship, or innovation.

- Abundant wealth can provide your family with a sense of security and stability, allowing them to pursue their dreams and passions without worrying about financial constraints.
- By creating abundant wealth in your family, you can help preserve and pass down your family's values and traditions to future generations.
- Wealth can provide your family with the resources they need to pursue personal growth and development, creating a legacy of self-improvement and lifelong learning.
- Abundant wealth can encourage generosity in your family, inspiring them to give back to their community and create a legacy of giving.
- Future generations will feel your legacy as a responsibility to be good people.
- Your success will inspire success in others.

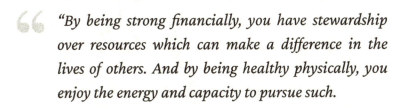 *"By being strong financially, you have stewardship over resources which can make a difference in the lives of others. And by being healthy physically, you enjoy the energy and capacity to pursue such.*

Early in my marriage, my wife and I overbought for our home. Prices were going up, and we were fearful that if we did not buy in then, we would never be able to afford one. Unknowingly, that decision tied us to a financial commitment (the house) that soaked up all our resources and arguably parts of our physical health. It precluded us from being generous. It precluded us from investing in our health. It required us both to work which soaked up a significant portion of our time. You get the picture.

After many years, we had the courage to sell the home and get into a less expensive home where we could also be generous and protect our own health. Looking back, this was an inflection point in not only our wealth building since then, but more importantly to us, the change of heart that comes from generosity (of both resource and time).

Today we find ourselves building on the practices of good financial stewardship through intentional budgets that align with our giving, saving, and life-style goals. Additionally, we have been part of a fitness community (boot camp) where we find accountability and like-minded individuals where we can protect and grow our physical health.

These habits have become routine for us now, and act as the continual fuel for us to pursue the best versions of ourselves."

— MATT MUNSON // FOUNDER OF SERVANT FINANCIAL LLC

ENCOURAGE ENTREPRENEURSHIP

Wealth can encourage entrepreneurship and innovation in your family, creating a legacy of creativity and responsible risk-taking.

My older four kids have each earned money by doing something they really enjoy, through advertising or by going door to door to get their own clients. It's been a great experience. Prior to heading off to play basketball at Brigham Young University, my oldest daughter McKinley was sponsored by Air Jordan. She was named one of the top 45 high school basketball players in the state of California! So for her business, she offered basketball skills clinics, coaching and training kids ages six through twelve. When she hosted those private clinics, she sometimes earned upwards of $100 to $150 an hour.

Teaching eight to ten kids to improve their basketball skills earned her much more than the alternatives of working at the movie theater or the hamburger restaurant and making thirteen bucks an hour. Plus, she learned to use her skills and talents to create greater financial success while doing something she truly enjoys.

My kids have learned from my example as an entrepreneur. Instead of going to a business that's hiring for an entry-level hourly wage position, they created their own neighborhood businesses. I love seeing creativity, innovation, and a growth mindset in action with young people. It's never too young to start.

Entrepreneurship takes who you are and magnifies it, instead of trying to fit into someone else's box. They're also not asking me if they can work at my company just because I'm their dad. Instead, my kids are figuring out what they personally love and are good at. The fact that I own a financial services company doesn't mean that's their industry. I want them to carve their own path.

My dad was not a business owner, but he was always a business leader and often the CEO where he worked. I never applied to work for him or at the companies he led, but instead decided to carve my own path too. I wanted to learn my own way and find out what I liked and was good at. I'm grateful he didn't pressure me to be just like him, and I plan to give that same gift to my kids. My wife and I will leave the legacy of encouraging our kids to build a life that makes them happy and to be the best at whatever they're striving to be. They can apply what we've taught them without feeling like they have to do exactly what we've done.

If you're an incredibly successful real estate investor and developer, that does not mean your kids are also fit to be incredibly successful in that same industry. You can teach them the principles and mindsets that made you successful and wealthy, encouraging them to apply those tools to their own interests and unique abilities, allowing them to find success in their own way.

My middle son, Sterling, has a great love of and skill with animals. We don't have dogs, but my sister and my parents each have dogs, and he's always loved them since he was little. At eleven or twelve years old, he decided to earn more money on his own by becoming a professional dog walker. He knew where all the dog owners lived in our neighborhood, and he made a flier that he dropped off by himself, going door to door on his scooter, knocking, and introducing himself. He offered to walk the dog thirty minutes a week or more. He got a few clients and increased the amount of time he could spend with animals, which is important to him. He also earns a lot of money for someone his age.

He learned interpersonal skills by talking to strangers about how to help them and what their dog's name, needs, and preferences are. He also needs to show up when he says he will, teaching him punctuality and follow through on his commitments. He's had to face rejection from people who aren't interested in his services. The whole experience is a hugely valuable way to learn.

> *"The purpose of life is not to be happy. It is to be useful, to be honorable, to be compassionate, to have it make some difference that you have lived and lived well."*
>
> — RALPH WALDO EMERSON

MAKING A POSITIVE IMPACT ON A BROADER SCALE

Health and wealth obviously benefit you as an individual, your family, your business, and your inner social circle. In the bigger picture, abundant wealth can make a positive impact in the community and the world.

I never ran for anything in school or served in any student body government positions. I was a captain of all the sports teams I played on, but I never was interested in the little clubs or politics.

However, as a business leader, I recognized a desperate need in my community for someone with investment expertise to serve as city treasurer and invest the large fund for taxpayers in our city. There was an open election in 2016, and a number of highly aggressive politicians were vying for that seat. I was recruited by some smart people who knew politics weren't my thing but financial expertise was, and they thought that could be the perfect combination to help the city. It wasn't about Republicans or Democrats, just the well-being of the whole municipality.

I publicly stay out of politics, but this elected position was neutral, so I agreed to learn more. I found that the elected position has an important responsibility of managing the investments for the city taxpayers to take care of firefighters, police, city employees, and their pensions. At the time, the account balance was $220 million. While I didn't have much time to give with my business and my family, I also didn't trust anyone else in the city to do a better job than I could. So I approached the position as community service.

When I announced my candidacy, influential political people told me I was too young and didn't know the game. They said I didn't have the connections, wasn't ready, and should wait for my time. It was sobering and alarming to see how politics works from the inside, but it also made me more determined to win, because I saw this old political guard wasn't focused on who would do the best job stewarding this money.

I used my business sense and campaigned completely differently from everyone else, spending a great deal of my own money. I held no fundraisers and pledged to give one hundred percent of my political salary to a Christian women's health charity, assisting women who can't afford healthcare, if I won.

I wanted the position because I was the most qualified person to hold it in my California city of 170,000 people. I was volunteering. Still, when I participated in debates, I got attacked. I was slandered online. People illegally ripped down my signs.

In the end, though, I won by an absolute landslide. I did such a good job that in 2020, no one ran against me. The account balance of the fund went from $220 million to $475 million. Our city went from being poorly rated financially to having the highest possible rating for a municipality. At the time of this writing, our city's investment fund is now worth $660 million.

Through this work, I can have a huge impact, and I've donated every penny I've earned for the last seven years to charity. Recently, I spoke to about three hundred people in the community about the financial progress and possibilities in our city. The person who introduced me said I was one of the area's most successful business owners. In the last eighty years, only politicians had held the position of city treasurer managing the investments, but he said for once, the city finally got it right by electing an investment advisor professional.

Most people in my shoes do not get involved in direct community service for the heck of it, but this position allows me to make a massive difference. I've been asked to run for Congress or Senate because of my reputation, background, and level of success. I've always declined because it would encroach on my family time. However, this position I'm currently in allows me to give back with the most impact and make a huge difference in the community, using my skills and abilities where they're most needed, not where they would most serve me.

 "What it means to be successful, and what I want my legacy to be, becomes clearer every day: honoring God, my family, and lifting up others. To get there specifically, creating and protecting freedom around time, money, relationships, and purpose have been core. They have been my life study for the past eighteen years, and the fruit of that effort is paying off in every way. My life is a series of small powerful habits stacked in such a way to make every day better and my future much brighter—not only for me, but for those causes and people I care about.

Today I get to enjoy better health, greater wealth, a richness of relationships that boggles my mind, and a fulfillment that I only dreamed of as a young man. I am extremely humbled and grateful."

— CHAD JOHNSON // FOUNDER OF
G5SUMMIT.COM

Serving the city without any personal financial gains is also a way to practice generosity, another principle we want to instill in our children. Abundant wealth gives you more freedom to do things for impact alone, without the need to get paid for it. And that in turn can encourage generosity in your family, inspiring them to give back to their community and create a legacy of giving.

My kids often come to the big community events and get to see their dad as an elected official, making an impact. People in the city will come up to my kids and tell them how much I've helped the community. As a result, they feel a sense of stewardship, pride, and responsibility. People know our family around here, and part of my legacy is the sense of responsibility my kids feel to be good, uphold our name, be generous, and be of service because of the path my wife and I have paved for them.

Think about these questions, and use them to guide your ridiculously ambitious goals and stay the course, even when the work is hard:

• What do you want your lasting mark on the world to be?

    – Write a two-paragraph obituary sharing what you want your close family and friends to remember you by.

    – Think of three causes you'd love to donate financial resources to in order to create a massive legacy.

    – Think about the possibilities of wealth transfer and what opportunities your success could create for the people you care about.

• What are you currently teaching future generations about health and wealth, and what do you want to teach them?

• What healthy habits would you love to see your family adopt as a result of your example?

CONCLUSION

My eighteen-year-old daughter McKinley recently wrote me a note about how it feels to have a motivated dad and how my example has impacted her life. It was very meaningful to me: "Having a motivated dad impacts me and my siblings and helps us have confidence and motivates us to be healthy and ambitious ourselves."

The process and keeping commitments to yourself are what's important. On my journey to write this book, I've learned we set our own limitations—or break through them. I thought losing fifty pounds sounded so cool. I really wanted to do it, but it also seemed totally impossible. And now as you read this, I sit fifty pounds lighter than the night I started writing this book.

I've also reinforced for myself the value of having the right experts. There's a zero percent chance I could have achieved this transformation by myself.

I've learned what a difference it makes when you see yourself transforming as a result of your own discipline. That process opens you up to other opportunities that are completely unrelated, because you see that discipline equals freedom and nothing is impossible.

When you finish this book, I hope you will not only be inspired but will also start on day one of newly committing to making an incredible impact on your life, the lives of your family, and your future legacy through creating optimal health and significant wealth. Both excellent health and significant wealth come only from a mindset of abundance and possibility.

The lessons of *Fit for Wealth* don't end here on this last page. They're your call to action, a nudge towards achieving both optimal health and immense wealth. One without the other is half-baked. If you optimize and achieve both, you'll have a much bigger impact and legacy than if you only focus on one. You can truly maximize your impact, ensure your legacy, and inspire those around you. So what are you waiting for? Now is your time.

ABOUT THE AUTHOR

Chad Willardson, CFF, CRPC®, AWMA®, is the President of Pacific Capital, a fiduciary wealth advisory firm he founded in 2011 that serves high net-worth entrepreneurs and families. He is the author of three best-selling books. His first book, *Stress-Free Money*, was featured in *Forbes*'s "21 Books To Read In 2021." His second book, *Smart Not Spoiled*, is increasing financial literacy among young people across the country and led to him co-founding the app GravyStack and co-hosting the Smart Money Parenting Show, which reached the #2 Podcast on Apple worldwide for Parenting, Kids & Family. His third and most recent book, *Beyond The Money*, is tailored to the eight-figure entrepreneurial clients Pacific Capital serves.

In addition to serving the family office clients of Pacific Capital, Chad manages a $660 million investment portfolio as the elected City Treasurer for the 170,000 residents in his community. Chad is recognized as one of the top wealth management experts in the country and has appeared in the *Wall Street Journal, Forbes, Inc., NBC News, CNBC, Yahoo Finance, Nasdaq, U.S. News & World Report, Investment News,* and *Financial Advisor Magazine*; he also writes for *Entrepreneur*. He has contributed to two bestselling books:

Who Not How and *The Gap and the Gain*, both by Dan Sullivan and Dr. Benjamin Hardy.

He earned his bachelor's degree in economics from Brigham Young University in Provo, Utah. Chad created and trademarked The Financial Life Inspection®, a unique process to remove people's stress about their money. Chad is passionate about financial education and believes that with the right tools and resources, people can be empowered to make smart money decisions. As a Certified Financial Fiduciary®, he loves to help people organize their financial life, clarify their goals, and make decisions that lead them to a successful and fulfilling life. As a father of five, teaching children to be smart and not spoiled is especially important to him.

Outside of his business, Chad loves to travel with his family and enjoys playing and watching sports. Chad and his family are very engaged in serving their community. Besides serving as an elected official, he and his family seek out ways to give back to various charitable causes. Chad served as a volunteer for two years on a church service mission in Lithuania, Latvia, Estonia, and Belarus and can speak, read, and write fluently in Lithuanian. Above all, Chad cherishes his family. A native of Orange County, California, Chad and his wife of twenty-two years live in Southern California with their five beautiful children.

NOTES

INTRODUCTION

1. Green, Nigel James. "The Deep Connection Between Your Health and Wealth." Forbes, July 2, 2020. https://www.forbes.com/sites/forbesfinancecouncil/2020/07/03/the-deep-connection-between-your-health-and-wealth/?sh=6543ceb952aa.
2. Friedman, Zack. "Shock Poll: 7 in 10 Americans Live Paycheck to Paycheck." Forbes, April 14, 2022. https://www.forbes.com/sites/zackfriedman/2022/02/08/shock-poll-7-in-10-americans-live-paycheck-to-paycheck/?sh=4a2b72ea55f6.
3. Mohabir, Melissa. "The 8 Scariest American Health Facts." Muscle & Fitness, November 4, 2019. https://www.muscleandfitness.com/features/active-lifestyle/8-scariest-american-health-facts/.

1. BE RIDICULOUSLY AMBITIOUS

1. Grinis, Leon. "No. 1 Fastest-Growing U.S. IP Firm Third Year in a Row." Caldwell, March 15, 2023. https://caldwelllaw.com/news/no-1-fastest-growing-ip-firm-third-year-in-a-row/.
2. Bienasz, Gabrielle. "Before Starting His Law Firm, He Narrowly Avoided Prison. Now He's Giving Back by Helping an Incarcerated Entrepreneur." Inc., December 23, 2021. https://www.inc.com/gabrielle-bienasz/caldwell-intellectual-property-law-firm-pro-bono-patent-work.html.

2. AVOID TEMPTATIONS

1. *The 100 Percent Rule That Will Change Your Life | Benjamin Hardy | TEDx-Klagenfurt. YouTube.* YouTube, 2019. https://www.youtube.com/watch?v=vj-91dMvQQo.

5. LEVERAGE THE COMPOUND EFFECT

1. *Simon Sinek on the Struggle of Balancing Service and Self. YouTube.* Capture Your Flag, 2022. https://www.youtube.com/watch?v=PQ6dbWxI5wE.

Printed in the USA
CPSIA information can be obtained
at www.ICGtesting.com
LVHW041326311023
762155LV00003B/3/J